John Wilkes

Three Interesting Tracts

Viz. I. Observations on the papers relative to the rupture with Spain. II. A letter to the electors of Aylesbury. III. A letter to His Grace the Duke of Grafton. Third Edition

John Wilkes

Three Interesting Tracts
Viz. I. Observations on the papers relative to the rupture with Spain. II. A letter to the electors of Aylesbury. III. A letter to His Grace the Duke of Grafton. Third Edition

ISBN/EAN: 9783337244040

Printed in Europe, USA, Canada, Australia, Japan

Cover: Foto ©ninafisch / pixelio.de

More available books at **www.hansebooks.com**

OBSERVATIONS ON THE PAPERS RELATIVE TO THE RVPTVRE WITH SPAIN,

LAID BEFORE BOTH HOVSES OF PARLIAMENT, ON FRIDAY THE TWENTY-NINTH DAY OF JANVARY, 1762, BY HIS MAJESTY's COMMAND.

IN A LETTER FROM A MEMBER OF PARLIAMENT, TO A FRIEND IN THE COVNTRY.

By *JOHN WILKES*, Esq;

THE THIRD EDITION.

Quis feræ
Bellum curet Iberiæ! HOR.

LONDON:

Printed for J. ALMON, opposite *Burlington-House, Piccadilly*. MDCCLXVII.

N. B. All the References in this Pamphlet are made to the Quarto Edition of the PAPERS, &c. delivered to the Members of both Houses of Parliament.

"After the omnipotence of lord "Bute in 1761 had forced Mr. Pitt "to retire from his Majesty's Coun-"cils, and the cause was declared "by himself to be our conduct rela-"tive to Spain, I had the happiness "of setting that affair in so clear and "advantageous a light, that he ex-"pressed the most entire satisfaction, "and particular obligations to my "friendship." *See Mr. Wilkes's Letter to the Duke of Grafton.*

OBSERVATIONS ON THE PAPERS RELATIVE TO THE RUPTURE WITH SPAIN.

DEAR SIR, *March* 9, 1762.

I Much regret that it is not yet in my Power fully to gratify the Curiosity you express of seeing *all the Papers relative to the Rupture with Spain.* The Subject is so very interesting, that I am not surprized at your Impatience. My Concern is, that so much is withheld from the Public, and that a Person, uninformed as I am, cannot pretend with Clearness to unravel the Thread of a Negociation, de-

 signedly

signedly kept intricate and embarrass-ed. I fear you will find some Things rather obscure; but I will endeavour to pour all the Light I can on the Subject, and to dissipate every Cloud of Obscurity which is meant to cover it. Had the Public been gratified with a Sight of the Memorials and Papers relating to the Demand of Liberty to the *Spanish* Nation to fish on the Banks of *Newfoundland* (*a Matter held sacred**), and to the other Claims,

* *You will* again *on this Occasion let M.* Wall *clearly understand, That this is a Matter held sacred; and that no Concession on the Part of his Majesty, so destructive to this true and capital Interest of* Great Britain, *will be yielded to* Spain, *however abetted and supported. Mr.* Pitt's *Letter*, p. 3. *With regard to the* Newfoundland *Fishery, M.* Wall *urged, What had principally given Offence here as to that Article, was my being so frequently ordered to declare, and the Conde* de Fuentes *having been as often told, that* England *would never hear of that inadmissible Pretension. Lord* Bristol's *Letter to the Earl of* Egremont, Dec. 6, 1761, p. 53.

The

Claims, equally unjust, made by the Count *de Fuentes*, which were moved for in the House of Commons on the 11th of *December* last, we might, with

The Declaration of the Count *de Fuentes*, that Mr. *Pitt*'s ordinary and last Answer was, " That he would not relax *in any thing*, till the Tower of *London* was taken Sword in Hand," p. 45. is undoubtedly a gross Misrepresentation. *That* Expression must have been confined to the Spanish *Claim of fishing on the Banks of Newfoundland*; for it is apparent from these *Papers*, than Mr. *Pitt* was ready to make greater Concessions to preserve the Friendship of *Spain*, that any former Minister had ventured to offer; witness the Paragraph in Lord *Bristol*'s Letter of *August* 31, p. 8. *Lastly, concerning the Disputes about the Coast of* Honduras, *I could add nothing to the repeated Declarations I had made in the King's Name, of the Satisfaction with which his Majesty would receive any just Overture from* Spain *(upon Condition that* France *was not to be the Channel of that Conveyance) for terminating amicably, and to mutual Satisfaction, every reasonable Complaint on this Matter, by proposing some equitable Regulation for securing to us the long-enjoyed Privilege of cutting Logwood (an Indulgence confirmed by Treaty, and of*

 course

with a tolerable Degree of Accuracy, have known ſomething more of the Merits of the preſent Quarrel with *Spain.* Not one of theſe appears, nor have we any Paper or Memorial from *Spain* (not even that delivered to Lord *Briſtol* in *January* laſt*), nor any Anſwer of the Court of *England*, ſince the Acceſſion of his preſent Catholic Majeſty (important as that Period muſt naturally ſeem to be) to the laſt Autumn. In vain have I wiſhed for the famous Memorial which the Court of *Spain* returned as inadmiſſible, that I might have com-

courſe authorized in the moſt ſacred Manner) ; nor could I give ſtronger Aſſurances than the paſt, of his Majeſty's ſteady Purpoſe to cauſe all Eſtabliſhments on the Logwood Coaſts, contrary to the Territorial Juriſdiction of Spain, *to be removed.*

* *Yet when the ſtile of General* Wall's *encloſed Paper is compared with that which was given to me laſt* January, *I hope it will appear there is leſs Peeviſhneſs at preſent here, than what was ſo ſtrongly exhibited ſome Months ago,* p. 11.

compared it with M. *de Buſſy*'s; ſince the late Miniſter publicly declared *that* was the precedent he followed with reſpect to the Memorial of *Spaniſh* Affairs given in by *France*. It is undoubtedly of much Conſequence to know both the *Matter and Expreſſions* of that Memorial returned by *Spain*, as it might probably relate to one of the three Points in Negociation, *Prizes*, *Logwood*, or the *Fiſhery*. In the preſent Collection (which was laid before both Houſes of Parliament on the 29th of *January*, but not Printed and delivered to the Members till the 12th of *Februry*), there is not a Line previous to the Memorial delivered to Mr. Secretary *Pitt*, by M. *de Buſſy*, *July* 23, 1761; nor is there any Intelligence from *Paris*, where the *Family Compact* of the Houſe of *Bourbon* was Negociated and ſigned by *Grimaldi*, and where, it is ſaid, the Meaſures to be taken againſt-

against *Portugal* were concerted. An EXTRACT of one Letter only of Mr. *Pitt*'s is inserted, which is dated *July* 28, the Answer to which is received *September* 11. Not a Syllable after that Period from this Court to Lord *Bristol*, till the 28th of *October*, when Lord *Egremont* declares he *opens his Correspondence*, p. 20*. It is indeed very astonishing, and gives no great Idea of the Vigilance or Attention of Administration, that while Affairs were so critical between the two Nations, no Directions for the Conduct

* How can this be the Truth, when Lord *Bristol* writes, *November* 16, 1761. *The Messenger* Ardouin, *delivered to me on the* 10*th Instant, at the* Escurial, *the Honour of your Lordship's Dispatches of the* 28*th past, with the several Enclosures therein referred to*; *and by the last Post* I RECEIVED YOUR LETTER OF THE 20th OF THE SAME MONTH, *in which your Lordship informed me, that all mine to the* 21*st of* September, *had been regularly laid before his Majesty*, p. 36. I suppose the Public could not be trusted with *all* that Letter.

duct of Lord *Bristol* were sent to *Madrid* during so long a Period *. But can it be imagined that so acute, so well-informed a Minister as Mr. *Stanley* certainly was, should not transmit from *Paris* any intelligence of that most alarming Treaty, which was negociating all the Summer at *Paris*? It appears by the Accounts published by the *French* Court, that the *Family Compact* was signed at *Versailles* the 15th of *August*, and ratified the 8th of *September*. LORD TEMPLE, in a great assembly, did declare that Intelligence of the highest Moment relative to these Matters was transmitted to this Court before the Advice in Writing, dated the 18th of *September*, which occasioned certain Resig-

* How is this to be reconciled to the Declaration of Lord *Egremont*, Mr. *Pitt*'s Successor, that the New Ministry *will avoid every possible Imputation of Indecision or Indolence, which ignorant Prejudice might suggest?* p. 23.

Resignations. Nothing of this kind is published in the *Papers relative to the Rupture with Spain*, though undoubtedly *Intelligence* constitutes a most material Part of those *Papers*. If we have not the Satisfaction of judging for ourselves from the *Whole* of a Case, I will do the late Minister the Justice to say, that it cannot be imputed to him. He pressed with honest Zeal the laying before the Public every Paper relative to the *six Years Negociation** with *Spain*, that the Justice and Candour of the Crown of *England* on the one hand, and the Chicanery, Insolence, and Perfidy of *Spain* on the other, might be apparent to all the World: But this was refused; for

* I should be particularly curious, for certain Reasons, to see in what Manner, and to what Extent, the *Spanish* Court *had been flattered by that of* London, *with an impartial Discussion of their Disputes, from the Year* 1754, before Mr. *Pitt* accepted the Seals, *p.* 53.

had

had it been granted, all the atrocius Calumnies ſo induſtriouſly circulated, of his Averſion to Peace, and his Endeavours to perpetuate and encreaſe the War, had been laid open to Mankind, and the Authors of them held in juſt Abhorrence. I own the Appeal to ſo much written Evidence, ſpoke to me the ſtrongeſt Language of Conſcious Integrity, and I was charmed with an Example, which I am ſure Mr. *Pitt* did not draw from any of his Predeceſſors in this Country.—They have ever ſought, like Mr. *Pitt's* Succeſſors, to cover and conceal, or at leaſt to perplex; he wiſhes to lay open and reveal to the unerring Public, both the motives and Actions of every Part of his Adminiſtration.—A Retroſpect carries no Terrors but to the Guilty—to an upright Miniſter it muſt give the trueſt Satisfaction—to the Public that Con-

Conviction it has in many Cases a Right to expect.

I was not a little surprised, and I own greatly concerned at the Alarm you mention, spread every where in your Parts, of the melancholy and ruined State of our Country, and the necessity we were under of accepting almost any Peace. *The French*, Lord *Bristol* says, *have never disconti-nued assuring the* Spaniards *of our being exhausted by the present long and expen-sive war*, p. 29: and they may add that we have those among us (but, happily for this Nation, they are few, and their Credit but small) who re-pine at our Successes, and declare they *weep over our Victories.* This is the true Picture of that most malignant and infernal Fiend, Envy, so well de-scribed by Ovid;

*Vixque tenet lacrymas, quia nil lacryma-
bile cernit.*

And

And a little before he mentions what rankled at the Heart;

Sed videt ingratos, intabescitque videndo
Successus hominis.

I doubt not these Men do very sincerely lament the Successes even of their own Country; for I well remember the favourite Language they held a few Years ago, "Give the "new Minister the Reins——he is "equally impracticable as impetuous "——in a very short Time he must "annihilate his present Credit with "the Public, from the Failure of "every Scheme he adopts." Now Heaven has given such glorious Success to upright Intentions, and well-digested * Plans, while the rest of their

* In *Europe*, *Cherbourg*, and *Belle-Isle*; in *Asia*, *Pondicherry*; in *Africa*, *Senegal*, and *Goree*; in *America*, *Beau Sejour*, *Louisbourg*, *Fort du Quesne*, now *Pittsburg*, *Guadalupe*, &c. *Niagara*, *Ticonderoga*, *Crown Point*, *Quebec*, *Montreal*, *Dominico*, and, to crown the whole, we may hope

 Marti-

their Countrymen are congratulating each other on all our noble Conqueſts and real Acquiſitions of Strength, theſe Men, as well as our declared Enemies, are found in Sorrow and Tears. How prepoſterous is ſuch a Conduct? Yet did not ſome of theſe very Men execrate thoſe as Traitors to their Country, who were not fired with Rapture at the Victory of *Culloden?* A Victory as juſtly dear to every Friend of Liberty as any our Annals can boaſt ——

But let us on the other hand exult, and rejoice to ſee how greatly this Country now figures in the unprejudiced Judgment of Foreigners, even of our Enemies. The Prime Miniſter of *Spain* tells Lord *Briſtol*, *That the Court of* London *was in the moſt flouriſhing and moſt exalted Situation*

Martinico. Let me add the Annihilation of the *French* Marine and Commerce. All during Mr. *Pitt*'s Miniſtry.

it

it had ever known, occcasioned by the greatest Series of Prosperities that any single Nation had ever met with, p. 10. Can we wonder after this, that so much Abuse, such gross Scurrility, on Mr. *Pitt*, appears in *Fuentes*'s Papers? Is it not the highest Panegyric? I am persuaded, had the *Direction* of the *British* Counsels been suffered to continue in the same Hands, the Name of *Pitt* had soon been as much dreaded at *Madrid* as it is at *Paris*, or as it is dear to his grateful Countrymen. I speak with the honest Warmth and Pride of an *Englishman*, who really feels with his Sovereign *the great and important Services* * of Mr. *Pitt*, and glories in seeing his Country recovered from the most abject State of Despair to such a Pitch of Grandeur and Importance, as to hold the first Rank among the Powers of *Europe*.

* Vide *London Gazette* of *Oct*. 10, 1761.

The other Report you mention, that the late Minister *courted a War with Spain*, will receive as full a Confutation from these Papers. I shall, from among many, produce only two Passages, but too express to admit the least Shadow of a Doubt. The first is from the Conclusion of the EXTRACT of the only Letter we have of Mr. *Pitt*'s in this garbled Collection. After the insolent Memorial of *France* relative to *Spain* was delivered here by M. *de Bussy*, *little short of a Declaration of a War in Reversion, and that not at a Distance*, Mr. *Pitt* writes to Lord *Bristol*, *In case, upon entering into Remonstrance on this Affair, you shall perceive a Disposition in M.* Wall *to explain away and disavow the Authorization of* Spain *to this offensive Transaction of* France, AND TO COME TO CATEGORICAL AND SATISFACTORY DECLARATIONS RELATIVELY TO THE FINAL INTENTIONS OF SPAIN, *your Excel-*

Excellency will, with Readineſs and your uſual Addreſs, adapt yourſelf to ſo deſirable a Circumſtance, and will open to the Court of Madrid *as handſome a Retreat as may be, in caſe you perceive from the* Spaniſh *Miniſter that they* SINCERELY *wiſh to find one, and to remove, by an* EFFECTUAL SATISFACTION, *the unfavourable Impreſſions which this Memorial of* France *has juſtly and unavoidably made on the Mind of his Majeſty*, p. 3, 4. Is this the Language of a Miniſter *who courts a War?* Is it not the Reverſe? Does he not honeſtly point out the Means of avoiding a War, yet with the Dignity and Spirit becoming a great Power, which did not tremble at the haughty Menaces of the *Spaniard?*

The other Paſſage contains the Teſminony of the Earl of *Egremont: M.* Wall *muſt himſelf know that there has been a particular Delicacy obſerved, in concerting our Plans for military Opera-*

tions, to avoid carrying Hostilities towards Objects, which might give the least Jealousy or Umbrage to the Court of Spain; *and therefore his Majesty can only consider such unjust Suggestions and groundless Suspicions, as destitute of Probability as of Proof, as a mere Pretext, in case that, contrary to all good Faith, and the most solemn repeated Professions of friendly Intentions, the Court of* Spain *should have meditated or resolved on Hostilities against* England, p. 31 *.

I think it appears to demonstration, *even from these Papers*, that before the first Overtures of *France* for the particular Peace with *England*, *Spain* had resolved, at a proper Time, to take an efficient and openly hostile Part against us. *M. de Bussy*, in the Memorial relative to *Spain*, so early as *July* 23,

* *Mr.* Wall *owned, how cautious we had been to avoid attacking those Possessions belonging to our Enemies, which had any Connection with the* Spanish *Territory.* Lord *Bristol*'s Letter, p. 63.

talks

talks *of the Engagements, which the one and the other Court may have taken prior to their Reconciliation*, p. 4. Mr. *Pitt's* Letter of *July* 28, declares, *The Duke* de Choiſeul *avows the Engagements with* Spain, *concerning our Diſputes with that Crown, to have been taken before the* FIRST OVERTURES *of* France *for the particular Peace with* England. The firſt Overtures were dated the 26th of *March*, 1761 *. Lord *Briſtol*, *Aug.* 31, gives an Account of the Converſation he had with General *Wall*, in which M. *Wall* declared, that M. *Buſſy's Memorial was Verbatim what had been ſent by Order of the Catholic King to* Verſailles, p. 6. † In the ſame

* Vide *Memoire Hiſtorique*, &c. publiſhed by the Court of *France*.

† In the Paper of the 28th of *Auguſt*, *Spain* with her uſual Perfidy *repeated in Anſwer*, *that ſhe only* conſented *that* France *ſhould take this Step*, p. 15. This is of a Piece with her Veracity, when ſhe ſays, *From a freſh Proof of his pacific Spirit*,

ſame Letter, p. 11. *The ſtrong Avowal of a moſt intimate Cordiality between* Spain *and* France *contained in this laſt Production of the* Spaniſh *Secretary of State has hurt me.* This Production was the famous Memorial of the 28th of *Auguſt*, which (with Lord *Briſtol's* Letter of the 31ſt, and an Encloſure) was the laſt Paper Mr. *Pitt* ever received from the Court of *Spain*; as appears from the Date of his Reſignation, *October* 5. *The Memorial which M.* de Buſſy *preſented to Mr.* Pitt, *is a Step,*

Spirit, the King of Spain *wrote to the King of* France, *his Couſin, that if the Union of Intereſt, in any manner retarded the Peace with* England, *he* conſented *to ſeparate himſelf from it, not to put* any Obſtacle *to ſo great a Happineſs*, p. 46. It is notorious in *France*, that *every Obſtacle poſſible* was put to it by the *Spaniſh* Miniſter, in Conjunction with the *Imperial*, at *Paris*, and in reality *Spain* only wiſhed not to *be* REPUTED *an Impediment to the Concluſion of a Peace between* England *and* France, p. 55. Another Proof of her Veracity may be ſeen in p. 44. of this Pamphlet.

Step, which his Catholic Majesty will not deny has been taken with his full Consent, Approbation, and Pleasure. Paper delivered to the Earl of *Bristol*, p. 13. which next holds out *mutual Assistance, as their Union, Friendship, and Relationship require:* then proceeds to a menacing Parallel, *It being grounded upon this, that if* England *saw that* France *attacked the Dominions of* Spain, *particularly in* America, *she would run immediately to her Defence for her own Conveniency, as well as because she had, equally with* France, *guarantied them:* and concludes with a Simile of obliging Delicacy betwixt crowned Heads, with regard to our Establishment on the *Logwood* Coast. *Hard Proceedings certainly, for one to confess that he is gone into the House of another, to take away his Jewels, and to say, "I will "go out again, but first you shall engage "to give me what I went to take."* So much

much for *becoming Apologies* * ! p. 16. *There is the greateſt Harmony between the two Courts* (France and Spain), p. 14. *Particularly ſince the King* (of Spain) *ſent your Excellency* (the Conde de Fuentes) *to that Court* (of London), *proving the inconteſtible Grounds of our Complaints and juſt Cares, and repeating that without ſatisfying them, it is impoſſible to fix the good Correſpondence of the two Monarchies, nor the Friendſhip of the two Monarchs*, p. 59. The Memorial itſelf preſented by *M. de Buſſy*, *July* 23, which was Verbatim ſent from *Spain*, threatens *a new War in* Europe *and* America, *if the Differences of* Spain *with* England *are not adjuſted, of which*, the *French* King ſays, *he ſhall be obliged to partake*, p. 4. And

* This Paper is ſtiled by *Spain*, a Memorial, p. 40, and contains thoſe *becoming Apologies*, on the Part of the Catholic Court, mentioned in the *Engliſh* Declaration of War. *Apologies* equally *becoming* and *convincing* !

in p. 39, General *Wall* says, *What other Discussion of the Matter of our Disputes, than what has been agitated, during so long a Negociation; what other Expedients can be found to save the Honour and Dignity of the two Kings, that have not been proposed and exhausted in a Contest of six Years?* And again, p. 40. *A Negociation so strongly discussed, that it has been reduced during your Embassy* (Count *de Fuentes's*) *to the last Yes, or to the last No.* In p. 60. *What greater Discussion, upon the Points of our Disputes, can be made, than that which has been in so long a Negociation? What Expedients can be fallen upon now to save the Honour of the two Kings, which in Arguments and Disputes of six Years have not occurred?* Lord *Bristol, Nov.* 2, writes, *I have* LONG *observed the Jealousy of* Spain *at the* British *Conquests* *, *and am now convinced, that the Con-*

* It is important to know in what Terms, and

Consciousness of this Country's Naval Inferiority has occasioned the * SOOTHING DECLARATIONS, *so repeatedly made, of a Desire to maintain Harmony and Friendship with* England, p. 29.

I be-

and at what Time, *Spain* first manifested this Jealousy; as also in what Terms, and at what Time, she renewed her *stale and inadmissible Claim to the Fishery, which,* M. *Wall* says, *all* Lord Bristol's *Instructions had run to declare their Claim to be*, p. 27.

* In the *London Gazette* of *Saturday, October* 10, 1761, which first announced Mr. *Pitt's* Resignation, (the Notice of which was purposely omitted the preceding *Tuesday*, for Reasons I will not now enter into) is an Article dated *Madrid, September* 4, *A Report having been lately spread here, upon the Arrival of the last Letters from* France, *as if there was Reason to apprehend an immediate Rupture between our Court and that of* Great Britain; *we understand, that the* Spanish *Ministers, in a Conversation which they had lately with the Earl of* Bristol, *Embassador Extraordinary from his* Britannic *Majesty, expressed their Concern thereat, and declared very explicitly to his Excellency, that* ON THE PART OF THEIR COURT, THERE WAS NOT

I believe I may even from these Premises take it as proved beyond Contradiction, that *Spain* had come to a final Resolution, and only waited for some

NOT THE LEAST GROUND FOR ANY SUCH APPREHENSIONS, AS THE CATHOLIC KING HAD, AT NO TIME, BEEN MORE INTENT UPON CULTIVATING A GOOD CORRESPONDENCE WITH ENGLAND, THAN IN THE PRESENT CONJUNCTURE.

General *Wall*, in relation to this, declares, p. 38. *I do not remember any thing, at this time, more particular, than on an infinite Number of other Occasions; neither do I myself comprehend the Motive for heightning this.* And again, p. 59. *I do not remember having made it then in a more particular manner than at many other times, neither do I comprehend the Motives for their making such a Point of it.* The motives for the *heightning* and *making such a Point of it*, are well understood at *London*, tho' not at *Madrid*. Mr. *Pitt* does not seem to have been the Dupe of these *soothing Declarations*, which were only the same Lord *Bristol* had just before given from M. *Wall*, in his Letter of the 31st of *August*. *His Catholic Majesty's Disposition and Professions had invariably been the same, and*

ſome favourable Events to throw off the Maſk of Deceit and Treachery. The Denouement quickly followed, tho' probably rather ſooner than *Spain* herſelf intended. Lord *Briſtol* explains the true Reaſons. In his Letter of *Sept.* 21, which was received here *Oct.* 16, he ſays, *A Meſſenger arrived at* St. Ildephonſo *laſt Week, with the News of the ſafe Arrival of the Flota in the Bay of* Cadiz, p. 17. In the Letter of *Nov.* 2. *Two Ships have lately arrived at* Cadiz, *with very extraordinary rich Cargoes from the* Weſt-Indies; SO THAT ALL THE WEALTH THAT WAS EXPECTED FROM SPANISH AMERICA IS NOW SAFE IN OLD SPAIN, p. 29. And again, p. 35. *Eleven large Ships of the Line, now*

were ever meant to cement and cultivate the Friendſhip ſo happily ſubſiſting between our two Courts, p. 11. Is it poſſible to think the Adminiſtration was deceived? or did they mean to deceive the Public?

lyin

lying at Ferrol, *are rigged, manned, and ready to put to Sea at a ſhort Warning, together with two Frigates, one of which is bound to the* South Seas, *with Cannon-ball, Powder, and many other Implements of War. By Advices from* Barcelona, *I hear that two of the Catholic King's Ships of War ſailed from thence the End of laſt Month, with two large Ships under their Convoy, loaded with* 3500 *Barrels of Gunpowder,* 1500 *Bomb-ſhells,* 500 *Cheſts of Arms, and a conſiderable Quantity of Cannon-balls of different Dimenſions, which Cargo, it is imagined, is deſtined for the* Spaniſh Weſt Indies. *Many more warlike Stores are ready to be ſhipped from* Catalonia. *Five Battalions of different Regiments of Infantry, and two Squadrons of Dragoons, are at* Cadiz, *waiting their final Orders to embark for* America. *This Corps makes in all about* 3,600 *Men,* p. 35. Lord *Egremont* ſays, *And his Majeſty having after-*

 wards,

wards, (that is, between the 31ſt of *Auguſt*, and the 28th of *October*) *received Intelligence, ſcarce admitting a Doubt, of Troops marching, and of military Preparations making in all the Ports of* Spain, *judged that his* DIGNITY, *as well as his Prudence, required him to order his Embaſſador at the Court of* Madrid, *by a Diſpatch dated the 28th of* October, *to demand*, &c. p. 48.

General *Wall*, thus prepared, at laſt comes out of his Intrenchments; for *Spain* no longer found her Account in *diſſembling*. She had already taken her Part, and the old Traffick of *Words* and *ſoothing Declarations* was almoſt at an End. On * *November* 2, (*eight* † Days

* This Letter cannot be too much attended to, as it ſtands immediately connected with the *Spaniſh* Paper or Memorial of the 28th of *Auguſt*, is explanatory of the real Purport of it, and evidently lays the Foundation of the Rupture, which the new Miniſtry have made with *Spain*.

† *The Meſſenger* Ardouin *delivered to me on the* 10th

Days before Lord *Bristol* received the very first * Dispatches from the new Ministry in *England.*) His Lordship writes Word of the *surprizing Change in General* Wall's *Discourse, and an unlooked-for Alteration of Sentiments, and complains of the haughty Language now held by this Court.* M. *Wall* declares *the Conduct of* England *unwarrantable, for his Catholic Majesty never could obtain an Answer to any Memorial or Paper—that we were intoxicated with our Successes—and that it was evident all we aimed at was, first to ruin the* French *Power, in order more easily to crush* Spain, *to drive all the Subjects of the Christian King, not only from their Island-Colonies in the new World, but also to destroy*

their

10*th Instant, at the* Escurial, *the Honour of your Lordship's Dispatches of the* 28*th past*, p. 36.

* The new Ministry never received any Answer to the Matter of these first Dispatches of the 28th of *October*, till the 24th of *December*, a Fortnight after the Rupture. Lord *Bristol*'s Letter, *December* 11, p. 41.

their several Forts and Settlements upon the Continent of North-America, *to have an easier Task in seizing on all the* Spanish *Dominions in those Parts, thereby to satisfy the utmost of our Ambition, and to gratify our unbounded Thirst of Conquest*; and afterwards, *that he would himself be the Man to advise the King of* Spain, *since his Dominions were to be overwhelmed, at least to have them seized with Arms in his Subjects Hands, and not to continue the passive Victim he had hitherto appeared to be in the Eyes of the World*, p. 26. Now what new Event, on the Part of *England*, since the Resignations, had happened to give Occasion to such a furious, futile, and menacing Declamation? Lord *Bristol* writes indeed, p. 64. *What had occasioned the great Fermentation during that Period at this Court, the Effects of which, I felt from General* Wall's *animated Discourse at the Escurial, was the Notice having, about that Time, reached the Catholic*

tholic King, that the Change which had happened in the English *Administration, was relative to Measures proposed to be taken against this Country:* But surely, almost in Lord *Egremont*'s own Words, p. 32, used by Lord *Bristol* himself to General *Wall, the Notoriety there was that every Thing in the Royal Councils, which could tend towards the Interruption of a friendly Intelligence between our Courts (which his Majesty was so solicitous to maintain) had also been avoided,* p. 62, with the consequential *Resignations,* must have produced in sound Argument a directly contrary Effect; whereas the Notice sent by his Lordship of the *Spanish* Preparations, and his other Reasonings, account very fully for the General's Animation at that Time.

I think the Question then is reduced to this short Point, *Does not the War with* Spain, *even in* September, *appear to have been unavoidable?* Most evidently

evidently ſo, from all the Proofs contained in the foregoing Pages, and even from what is given us of Lord *Briſtol*'s Letters, in particular that of *Auguſt* 31, with the Memorial incloſed, which was received here *September* 11, and was, to be ſure, no ſmall Part of the Ground, on which Lord *Temple*'s and Mr. *Pitt*'s written Advice of *September* 18, to recal Lord *Briſtol*, was founded. Every Practice of the moſt civilized States, every Formality preſcribed by the Law of Nations, every Proceeding which the moſt ſcrupulous Rules of good Faith, could require, might have been obſerved, and the nobleſt Opportunity of expeditiouſly and gloriouſly terminating both a *French* and a *Spaniſh* War been ſeized, which is now irrecoverably loſt. The firmeſt Nerves of *Spain*, and with them the laſt Hopes of *France*, might ſoon have been withered, and the *Britiſh* Empire have received

ceived greater, and more important, Acquiſitions, than any it yet can boaſt from the unparalleled, and dazzing Succeſſes, even of this glorious War.

Whoever conſiders the ſituation of *Spain* (unprepared as ſhe was at the time the written Advice was given *) with reſpect to her Ports, her Ships of War in thoſe Ports, her Colonies, her Comerce, her own as well as the Riches

* All Advices concur in proving, that the State of *Spain* was at that Time much the ſame as at the breaking out of the War in 1739. *The City of* Manila *might be well ſuppoſed to have been in the ſame defenceleſs Condition with all the other* Spaniſh *Settlements, juſt at the breaking out of the War: That is to ſay, their Fortifications neglected, and in many Places decayed; their Cannon diſmounted, or uſeleſs, by the mouldring of their Carriages; their Magazines, whether of military Stores or Proviſion, all empty; their Garriſons unpaid, and conſequently thin, ill-affected, and diſpirited; and the Royal Cheſts in* Peru, *whence alone all theſe Diſorders could receive their Redreſs, drained to the very Bottom.* Anſon's Voyage, Quarto Edition of 1748, p. 3.

of

of *France* on board her Ships, can never ſufficiently lament the Loſs of an autumnal Campaign *. If we add that the Fleet of *England* was at no Time ſo formidable, her Seamen never ſo full of Spirit, and fluſhed with repeated Victories, in *Europe* only upwards of 140 Ships of War, in the other Parts of the World above 100 more, we muſt ſink in Amazement at our Supineneſs and Neglect of ſo critical a Period, after ſo long Tameneſs under Injuries. I will add *long Tameneſs under Injuries*; for I think the Conduct of *Spain*, even during the ſix Years Negociation, was ſo groſsly partial to our profeſſed Enemies, as would have juſtified any overt Acts on the Side of *England*, from every Principle of Juſtice; but Motives of Moderation and Policy reſtrained us. The

* Part of the Preparations ſince made both in *Europe* and *America*, may be ſeen from Lord *Briſtol's* Teſtimony, p. 23, of this Pamphlet.

Affair

Affair of the *Antigallican* was alone of ſuch Magnitude, as to have called for Repriſals againſt a Court, which avowed ſuch groſs Partiality and Injuſtice, and committed ſuch repeated Acts of the higheſt Indignity. Not the leaſt Satisfaction was ever offered, though often demanded. On the contrary, it was followed by many flagrant Acts of notorious Violence. It is a known Fact, that both the Law of Nations, and the eſtabliſhed Cuſtoms of all Maritime States, have been violated by *Spain* in every one of her Ports, from a declared Partiality to the *French*. They were treated almoſt as natural-born *Spaniards*, tho' the *Family Compact* did not at that Time ſubſiſt, and the *Engliſh* as Enemies, tho' called Friends, to whom the King of *Spain* was ever declaring much Cordiality and Regard.

Ruinous indeed it may prove for this Country, that the Adminiſtration,

-tion, which for ſo many Years has continued UNANIMOUS in carrying on the War in *Germany*, UNANIMOUS likewiſe in rejecting the Terms of Peace offered by *France*, ſhould have differed in Opinion (if indeed they did ſo) with regard to the glaring Duplicity, and hoſtile Intentions, of the Court of *Spain!* It required alas! no great Scope of Judgment, nor any deep Sagacity, to diſcover the *real Views*, p. 24. of *Spain*, and that the War with that Power was inevitable. A Truth which moſt plainly appears from the very Papers publiſhed to conceal it. The only Queſtion moſt evidently was, whether we ſhould enter into it with every Advantage on our Side, or from Weakneſs, Indeciſion, or a deluſive Hope at beſt, give to our determined Enemy that Time to prepare, which it was notorious ſhe wanted, loſe the Seaſon for Action, and ſacrifice to the Imbecility of a few

more

more last Words three most important Months, at the End of which we find ourselves reduced to the Necessity of breaking with *Spain*, exactly as we ought to have done so long before. Whoever can now pride himself in the *procrastinating Advice* he gave to his Sovereign, may he enjoy in full Lustrè *that eminent Glory of his Life!* If such are the *Glories*, what must the *Disgraces* be! I mean not to draw any uncandid Picture of the present Administration: I am sorry I must say, that we have had too much Experience of one Part of them, and too little of the other, to be very sanguine. Two S——s. of S——e, in these dangerous Times, become Ministers by Inspiration! We have as little Experience of them, as they have of Business. In no Department of the State, nor in Parliament, has either held any Rank or Estimation. But these Defects will be amply supplied

 by

by the Induſtry and Experience of *a laborious Gentleman,* who has *long paced in the Trammels of the State,* with *no Ambition or Avarice to gratify.* A Declaration the Public has heard repeatedly from himſelf. He neither

Ambitione mala, aut argenti pallet *amore.*
HOR.

But may the Dignity of the Crown, the Honour of his Majeſty, the Glory of the Nation, and the important Acquiſitions made during the late Miniſtry, be ſafe in their Hands! Their Hands have been ſtrengthened in every manner they could aſk or wiſh; and no Oppoſition has been made to them; unleſs it is call'd Oppoſition, to endeavour to preſerve the Confidence of our Allies once boundleſs, and to keep up the high Spirit of the Nation under the enormous, but neceſſary, Burthens of the War.

In

In no truly *Britiſh* Quarrel, but in the Cauſe of our Allies, the *Spaniſh* Marine was deſtroyed by Sir *George Byng*, in 1718, without any previous Declaration of War. We were not, in conſequence of that Step, treated in *Europe* as an uncivilized Nation, ſpurning at all Laws, or as a Neſt of Pirates; but the *Policy* and *Spirit* of the Meaſure was univerſally admired. As to the *Juſtice* of ſuch a Proceeding, I determine nothing: I leave it to thoſe *State Caſuiſts* who ſeized the *French* Ships before a Declaration of War*. The Intereſt of *Great Britain* was not then immediately concerned, as in the preſent Caſe, but our Allies wiſhed, and obtained, our vigorous and effectual Support. By that deciſive Exertion of our Strength, the Conteſt between the two Nations, was in Effect finiſhed almoſt as ſoon as begun. The impartial Public will

* Vid. *Memoire Hiſtorique*, No. 17. Art. 12.

judge for themſelves, how great the Probability is, that the like Succeſs had followed Meaſures equally ſpirited, *preceded by a Declaration of War, which in this Caſe had been founded on the cleareſt Principles of Juſtice and Equity.* I am at leaſt certain no Man of Candour could have cenſured *England as accelerating precipitately a War* *, long reſolved by *Spain*, I muſt ſay, too long delayed by *England.* I rather fear *the Example of the Spirit of the late Meaſures* † will be thought to be already forgot; and as thoſe Meaſures were decried as too bold and daring, more feeble, more puſilanimous, leſs encouraging to our real Friends, leſs hoſtile to our Enemies, will be found to be adopted. In the preſent Caſe, Lord *Briſtol* is ordered, ſo early as *July* 28, *to come to categorical and ſatisfactory Declarations relatively*

* Vid. *the Declaration of War againſt* Spain, *Jan.* 2, 1762.

† Vid. *Lord* Egremont's *Letter*, p. 23.

tively to the final Intentions of Spain, *Mr.* Pitt's *Letter*, p. 3. to which Lord *Bristol*, on the Part of *Spain*, never returns either a CATEGORICAL or SATISFACTORY Answer. The *ingenuous* General *Wall*, through the whole Negociation, appears reserved and artful at least, not to say full of *Duplicity*. *At last General* Wall *replied, He had no Orders to acquaint me with any Measures but what he had formerly communicated to me; and signified his not being at Liberty to say any more*, Nov. 2. p. 27. *All that I could, with Difficulty, extort from General* Wall *was, that his Catholic Majesty had judged it expedient to renew his* FAMILY COMPACTS (*those were the express Words*) *with the Most Christian King — Here the* Spanish *Minister stopt short, and, as if he had gone beyond what he intended, he said, that the Count* de Fuentes, *and M.* Bussy, *had declared to his Majesty*'s *Ministers all that was* MEANT *to be*

 commu-

communicated to them, Nov. 2. p. 29. Can any thing be imagined more contemptuous, or more insolent? But what follows is excellent *Spanish* Humour, and the inimitable *Hogarth* could, from these few Lines, give us a most diverting Frontispiece to the *Papers*, if Administration did not seem resolved no more to employ Men of superior Parts and Genius. Lord *Bristol* says, *I began to flatter myself I might obtain the categorical Answer, I was ordered to demand, without the* Spanish *Minister's suspecting my ultimate Orders. When I was going out of his Room, he took me by the Hand, and said, with a* SMILE, *he* HOPED; *but there he stopped. I asked him what he* HOPED, *that I might also* HOPE, *and that all might concur in the same* HOPES: *But his Excellency only then bowed, and took his Leave of me*, p. 63. General *Wall* is too much of a *Spaniard* ever to *laugh*; but his *Smiles* are very significant.

cant. Lord *Bristol* declares, *M.* Wall *ever acted in too ingenuous a Manner for me to suspect the least Duplicity in his Conduct*, p. 19. Now was he ever *ingenuous* and frank enough to communicate to Lord *Bristol*, the least Article of the *Family Compact*, or did he ever hint that such a Thing was in Agitation? From *the Catholic King's very particular Partiality towards Lord* Bristol, p. 66. I suppose M. *Wall* was ordered to spare his Lordship the Concern so alarming a Treaty must have occasioned, and only, from time to time, to use the soothing Sounds of *Friendship*, *Honour*, *Cordiality*, *Affection*, &c. &c. to *smile*, to *bow*, to *take him by the Hand*, and to —— *hope*: What? I know no more than the present Ministry.

Lord *Bristol* seems totally uninformed of so important an Affair as the *Family Compact*, till long after that Treaty was signed and ratified, and only

only a few Days * before he is told of it from *England*. *October* 28, Lord *Egremont* writes to Lord *Bristol*: *His Majesty cannot imagine that the Court of* Spain *should think it unreasonable to desire a Communication of the Treaty* ACKNOWLEDGED *to have been lately concluded between the Courts of* Madrid *and* Versailles, p. 21. When was this *Acknowledgment* made? Surely *this* relates to the *Rupture* with *Spain*? Yet not a Line of this Intelligence is among the *Papers*.

By this Time, I think it must appear how much Lord *Bristol*, though possessed of real Talents, was deceived by the Court of *Spain*; a Court as insidious as that of *France*. Let me next remark, how dextrous the new Ministry here were in endeavouring to deceive themselves. In the Answer delivered to the Count *de Fuentes*, by the Earl of *Egremont*, *Dec*. 31, it is

* Vide his Letter of *Nov*. 2.

said,

ſaid, *The Embaſſador at the Court of* Madrid, *by a Diſpatch dated the 28th of* October, *was ordered to demand, in Terms the moſt meaſured, however, and the moſt amicable, a Communication of the Treaty recently concluded between the Courts of* Madrid *and* Verſailles, *or, at leaſt, of the Articles which might relate to the Intereſt of* Great Britain*—and—* TO CONTENT HIMSELF WITH ASSURANCES, *in caſe the Catholic King offered to give any, that the ſaid Engagements did not contain any thing that was contrary to the Friendſhip which ſubſiſted between the two Crowns, or that was prejudicial to the Intereſts of* Great Britain, *ſuppoſing that any Difficulty was made of ſhewing the Treaty*, p. 48. The new Miniſtry are now got off from the true Ground, which was the Memorial of *Spaniſh* Affairs *verbatim ſent from* Madrid, and the Letter of Lord *Briſtol*'s of *Auguſt* 31, with the Encloſures; and have confined their View

to

to the ſingle Point of the late Treaty, or the *Family Compact*. Every Thing relative to the *final Intentions* of *Spain*, concerning which Lord *Briſtol* is ordered, in Mr. *Pitt*'s Letter, ſo early as *July* 28, *to come to categorical and ſatisfactory Declarations*, is omitted in this Demand, and Lord *Briſtol* is ordered to confine himſelf to the new Treaty. This I agree with Lord *Egremont*, is certainly no *equivocal Proof of Dependance on the good Faith of the Catholic King, in ſhewing him an unbounded Confidence in ſo important an Affair*, p. 49: How merited, we have ſeen from what paſſed in the latter Months of the Negociation; and in all Probability ſhould ſee more glaringly, if the whole Negociation, ſince the Acceſſion of his preſent Catholic Majeſty, were communicated to us. From that *unbounded Confidence* the new Miniſtry entirely loſt Sight of the moſt offenſive and hoſtile Matter in the Me-

morial

morial of *July* 23, and the Papers of *August* 31, attacking the Dignity of the Crown of *England* in a manner ſurely far more unbecoming and inſolent than that *Spirit of Haughtineſs and Diſcord, which,* ſays M. *Wall, dictated that inconſiderate Step, and which, for the Misfortune of Mankind, ſtill reigns ſo much in the* Britiſh *Government, which made in the ſame Inſtant the Declaration of War, and attacked the King of* Spain'*s Dignity,* p. 67. It is plain they were accommodating themſelves at any rate tamely to become the Dupes to *Spain*; for all they deſired, by the Diſpatch of the 28th of *October*, was an Aſſurance of the *Innocence of the Treaty in Queſtion*, p. 23. and they paſſed by every Thing elſe, though of the moſt hoſtile Tendency. Conſcious of this, Lord *Egremont*, at the End of his Anſwer to the Conde *de Fuentes, December* 31, pleads guilty for himſelf and his Brother Miniſters,

to

to the Charge that may be exhibited againſt them of an intentionally facile and willing Credulity, when he ſays, *But fortunately the Terms in which the Declaration* * *(Fuentes's) is conceived, ſpare us the Regret of not having receiv-ed it ſooner; for it appears, at firſt Sight, that the Anſwer is not at all conformable to the Demand. We wanted to be in-formed, if the Court of* Spain *intended to join the* French, *our Enemies, to make War on* Great Britain; *or to depart from their Neutrality? Whereas the Anſwer concerns one Treaty only,* (all that was aſked by the Diſpatch of the 28th of *October,*) *which is ſaid to be of the* 15*th of* Auguſt; *carefully avoiding to ſay the leaſt Word that could explain, in any man-ner, the Intentions of* Spain *towards* Great Britain, *or the further Engage-ments*

* *That the ſaid Treaty is only a Convention be-tween the Family of* Bourbon, *wherein there is no-thing that has the leaſt Relation to the preſent War.* *Fuentes's* Note delivered to Lord *Egremont, Dec.* 25. p. 46.

ments they may have contracted in the present Crisis. In the Dispatch indeed of Lord *Egremont* to Lord *Bristol*, of *November* 19, in Answer to Lord *Bristol's* Letter of *November* 2, p. 32, the new Ministry amend their own Question, and at last demand *a* PRECISE *and* CATEGORICAL ANSWER *from the Court of* Madrid, *relative to their Intention with regard to* Great Britain *in this critical Conjuncture,* which brought on the Rupture on the 10th of *December*, and is precisely what was directed by Mr. *Pitt* so early as *July* 28.

I cannot pass by *that other* Part of Lord *Egremont's* Answer delivered to the Count *de Fuentes December* 31, in which it is said, *the Embassador* (of England) *having addressed himself to the Minister of* Spain *for that Purpose, could only draw from him a Refusal, to give a satisfactory Answer to his Majes-*

ty's JUST REQUISITIONS*, *which he had accompanied with Terms that breathed nothing but Haughtineſs, Animoſity, and Menace, and which ſeemed ſo ſtrongly to verify the Suſpicions of the unamicable Diſpoſition of the Court of* Spain, p. 49, without obſerving that this cannot poſſibly be the real State of the Fact, (though his Lordſhip but a few Lines before ſays, he *will confine himſelf to Facts, with the moſt ſcrupulous Exactneſs*) for Lord *Egremont* receives no Anſwer from Lord *Briſtol*

* The following Paragraph of Lord *Briſtol's* Letter of *Nov.* 2, p. 25, demonſtrates that theſe *juſt Requiſitions* were not made in conſequence of any Orders from the Court of *England: Such ſtrong Reports of an approaching Rupture between* Great Britain *and* Spain, *grounded upon ſeveral authentic Aſſurances I had received, that ſome Agreement had been ſettled and ſigned between their Catholic and Moſt Chriſtian Majeſties,* DETERMINED ME *to enquire minutely into this Affair.*

* to the Orders to make the JUST REQUISITIONS contained in his two Dispatches (of the 28th of *October*, and 19th of *November*,) till the 24th of

Decem-

* It is remarked in the Gazette of *Madrid*, published by Authority, in these Words: *And what is more singular, is, that they attribute the last Endeavour, which they ordered Lord* Bristol *to make, and which caused the Rupture, to the Language of Haughtiness, Animosity, and Menace, with which (according to them) our Court answered to the civil and amicable Demand that Minister made in Consequence (say they) of an Order of the* 28th *of* October. *Unfortunately for them, they have not considered that in an Interval from the 28th of* October *to the 1st or 2d of* December, *the Day upon which Lord* Bristol's *last Letter arrived, it is impossible an Express can come from* London *to* Madrid, *return to* London *with an Answer to his Dispatch, and go back to* Madrid *with the Reply.* Gazette de Amsterdam du Mardi 23 Février 1762. De Madrid le 2 Février 1762. Par le même courier, qui a apporté au Roi la nouvelle de la résolution prise à la cour *Britannique* de nous déclarer la guerre, le Comte de Fuentes a envoyé a S. M. un Mémoire remis à cet Ambassadeur avant son départ de Londres par le Comte d'E-gremont,

December, a Fortnight after the Rupture, which happened on the 10th, p. 41, & 43, except what I will now ſtate, which is far from containing the *repeated and the moſt ſtinging Refuſals to give the leaſt Satisfaction*, p. 50. Extract from Lord *Briſtol*'s Letter to the

gremont, Sécrétaire d'Etat de S. M. Britannique, en reponſe à la declaration que le Comte de Fuentes lui avoit donné par écrit quelques jours auparavant. Ces deux pieces ont été inſereés, par ordre de notre cour, dans la Gazette de Madrid, avec les obſervations ſuivantes ſur le memoire delivre par le Comte d'Egremont. —— *Et ce qu'il y a de plus ſingulier, c'eſt qu'ils attribuent la derniere tentative qu'on a fait faire au Lord Briſtol, et qui a cauſé la rupture, au ton de hauteur, d'animoſité, et de menace, avec lequel (ſelon eux) notre cour a repondu aux demandes honnétes et amiables que ce Miniſtre fit en vertu (diſent-ils) d'un ordre du 28 Octobre. Malheureuſement pour eux, ils n'ont point fait attention que, dans un intervalle comme celui du 28 du dit mois au* 1er *ou* 2. *de Decembre, jour auquel arriva le dernier courier du Lord Briſtol, il eſt impoſſible qu'on exprès vienne de Londres à Madrid, retourne à Londres avec la reponſe à ſa dépéche, et revienne a Madrid avec la replique.*

the Earl of *Egremont*, *November* 23, p. 37: *It will not be possible for me to re-dispatch a Messenger to* England *for several Days, notwithstanding my having had another long Conference with* M. Wall, *at which I entered minutely into every Argument suggested to me by your Lordship. Altho' I dare not flatter myself with having gained any Ground upon the Spanish Minister, yet I never before observed his Excellency listen with greater Attention to my Discourse, than at our late Meeting. When he answered me, it was without Warmth; when he applied to me, it was friendly; and, after long Reasonings, on both Sides, we parted with reciprocal Protestations to each other of our earnest Desire to continue in Peace. General* Wall *also promised me, to acquaint his Catholic Majesty circumstantially, with what had passed beeween us. I entreat your Lordship not to think me inconsequential in what I relate: It is my Duty to mention the Result of each In-*

terview with the Spaniſh *Secretary of State. All I ſent an Account of in my Letters of the 2d Inſtant, was literally what had happened at that Time; and the Change I have juſt hinted, when I laſt ſaw M.* Wall, *is equally certain.*

I will obſerve but upon one Paſſage more, and that is from Lord *Egremont*'s Diſpatch of *November* 19, becauſe when he is drove to the Neceſſity of defending the Proceedings of the preſent Miniſtry, he gives (what poſſibly was not his Object) the fulleſt Juſtification of Mr. *Pitt. As to the Aſſertion of that Miniſter (M.* Wall) " That his Catholic Majeſty never " could obtain an Anſwer from the " *Britiſh* Miniſtry, to any Memorial " or Paper that was ſent from *Spain*, " either by the Channel of the Count " *de Fuentes*, or through your Hands," *it would be a uſeleſs Condeſcenſion to appeal ſo repeatedly to thoſe ample Materials in your Excellency's Poſſeſſion, for the Confutation*

futation of a Propoſition ſo notoriouſly groundleſs, that it ſcarce deſerves a ſerious Anſwer. The Language M. Wall *held, relative to the late Negociation with* France, *as well as with regard to our Ambition and unbounded Thirſt of Conqueſt, as it conſiſts of mere abuſive Aſſertion, without the leaſt Shew of Argument, deſerves nothing but plain Contradiction,* p. 31.

Before I quit the *Papers*, it may be neceſſary to add, that I ſee nothing ſo alarming in the War with *Spain*, had it been entered into in Time, and were well conducted. I have read the Hiſtories of both Nations, and am happy to agree with our Miniſters, that *Experience has ſhewn, that when in Contradiction to the obvious Principles of our common Intereſts, that Harmony has been unhappily interrupted,* Spain *has always been the greateſt Sufferer,* p. 21. Need I do more in Support of this Opinion, than mention the late War againſt the com-

combined Forces of *France* and *Spain*, united before the *French* Marine was annihilated, as it now is, and at a Period, when the Navy of *England* had not reached its preſent Greatneſs, and irreſiſtible Superiority?

The Evidence to be drawn from theſe imperfect and mutilated Papers, is now fully and fairly ſtated. I call them *imperfect* and *mutilated*, becauſe they have their Commencement, only from the very Point, when the long Negociation between *England* and *Spain* being become hopeleſs, the inſolent Attempt was made by the two Branches of the Houſe of *Bourbon*, then united, to force on his Majeſty and the *Engliſh* Nation, the Conceſſion of thoſe inadmiſſable Terms, which *Spain* alone deſpaired of being able to compel us to *grant*. An Attempt of inſiduous Perfidy, which at once proved the particular Peace, betwixt *England* and *France* to be hopeleſs and impracti-

impracticable; for what Cessions to *France* could an *English* Administration be justified in making, while she declared herself eventually engaged to take part with *Spain* in a new War for *Spanish* Objects, totally inadmissible; from which Protest it doth not appear that either Court ever departed? The specious and false Appearances of Candour, which the Publication of *Papers* in such a State is meant to convey, are as easily seen thro' and detected, as they are unfair and ungenerous. A great deal of very important Intelligence, relative to the Point in Question, is plainly with-held. The Suspicions arising from the Suppression of Evidence are, no doubt, in the Opinion of Government, more tolerable than the Conviction founded upon full Proof. Even the Particulars of the *Negociation with France* are still secreted from the Public, as far as it is in the Power of *our Government*;

lest,

left, among other good Reasons, as it stands naturally connected with the *Spanish*, they might, if considered together, throw too striking a Light on the Whole. The infinite Importance of what is suppressed, I do not pretend to determine; but the *Papers* are evidently thus partially laid before the Public by Administration, to justify, if possible, their *Delay*; with what Success the Public will determine. As to the Wisdom of the *written Advice*, it stands already proved by the Event: but before we can enter fully into that Dispute (if there can be still a doubt) *all* the Materials, *all* the Evidence, both from *Papers* and *Facts*, on which *that Advice* was founded, ought, in common Justice, to be laid before the Public. From what we already know with Certainty, *even from these Papers*, as to *what* Spain *had already done*, *not from what that Court might further intend*

to

to do *, I cannot but own my Surprize, that there ſhould be *a Difference of Opinion with regard* to *Meaſures to be taken againſt* Spain, *of the higheſt Importance to the Honour of the Crown, and to the moſt eſſential National Intereſts**. When I am told that only one noble Lord, and the late Secretary of State, of the moſt confidential Servants of the Crown, concurred in an Opinion ſo evident, ſo clearly deduced from ſuch a Variety of Proofs, I cannot but imagine that there muſt have been ſome powerful Combination, ſome underhand Intrigues, among Miniſters of more Denominations than one, to force the Reſignation of the Right Hon. Gentleman. He muſt long have been looked upon with an unfriendly and jealous Eye by Miniſters, to whom it is his Honour that he was ſo very unlike; and who, though real

* *Vide* A Letter from a Right Hon. Perſon to ——— in the City.

Una-

Unanimity attended it in the Nation, could ill brook his poſſeſſing in ſo high a Degree, (what they never had the leaſt Share of) the Confidence of a diſcerning and enlightened People. A Point of the utmoſt Conſequence to every Miniſtry, in this Kingdom. The Glories of this Gentleman's Adminiſtration, (that is, while he *was allowed to guide* * *the Meaſures* of this Nation)

* If one Miniſter on *reſigning the Seals* may not, in the true Spirit of the Conſtitution, ſay that he reſigns, *in order not to remain reſponſible for Meaſures, which he was no longer allowed to guide* in his own Department, to the Execution of which he muſt ſet his Hand; what an Idea of Parliament and of the Conſtitution muſt another have entertained, who could, juſt before taking the Seals, write the following circular Letter, not yet *be-verſified*, or *be-noted?*

" SIR,

" The King has declared his Intention to " make me Secretary of State, and I (very un- " worthy as I fear I am of ſuch an Underta- " King)

Nation) and the Applauſes of his grateful Country, have given him at leaſt a due Portion of *Envy*, which is a certain Attendant on ſplendid Merit.

Sure Fate of all, beneath whoſe riſing Ray,
Each Star of meaner Merit fades away!
Oppreſs'd we feel the Beam directly beat;
Thoſe Suns of Glory pleaſe not till they ſet.
POPE.

That only two Reſignations have accompanied that of the late Secretary, is no Surprize to me.

Je ſuis Anglois, je dois faire le bien
De mon pays, mais plus encore le mien,

ſays *Voltaire*, who lived a good while in this Country, and ſeems to know it pretty well.

" king) *muſt take the Conduct of the Houſe of Com-*
" *mons.* I cannot therefore well accept the Of-
" fice till after the firſt Day's Debate, which
" may be a warm one. A great Attendance
" that Day of my Friends will be of the great-
" eſt Conſequence to my future Situation, and
" I ſhould be extremely happy, if you would,
" for that Reaſon, ſhew yourſelf amongſt them,
" to the great Honour of, *&c.*"

From these few and scanty Materials, so sparingly dealt out to the Public, I have endeavoured to give you all the Satisfaction in my Power. I could possibly have amused you more, but I have all along preferred the Desire of *informing* to that of *entertaining* you. Perhaps you had been better pleased, if I had deviated more, and had not confined myself so strictly to the Evidence of the *Papers*, and to *Facts* which will not be denied.

To conclude, Let me add to Hopes not very sanguine, very sincere and very fervent Wishes: *May the most perfect Harmony, mutual Confidence, and Unanimity, which*, Lord *Egremont*, *October* 28, says, p. 23, *now Reign in his Majesty's Councils*, for the sake of the Public, long continue! May the Expedition now sailed to the *West-Indies* prove, by Success, to have been timely in Preparation, adequate in Force, to the Object, whatever it may

may be! May our Army in *Germany**, (ſince it is ſtill to continue there, tho' Mr. *Pitt* is retired,) and the Kings of *Pruſſia* and *Portugal* find that *Example* has indeed been taken *of the Spirit of the late Meaſures* *, p. 23. and *that the Meaſures of Government will ſuffer no Relaxation*, p. 22. from feeble, procraſtinating, and undecided Counſels, founded in Weakneſs and Duplicity, and, to grace the Whole, may the beſt-diſpoſed Prince, that has at any Time ſwayed the Sceptre of *Alfred*, never live to want a Miniſter as able, and ſucceſsful as Mr. *Pitt*.

I am, &c.

* It is confidently aſſerted in Honour of the Secretary of State of the Northern Department, that *he likewiſe* did immediately on Mr. Pitt's Reſignation give the ſtrongeſt Aſſurances to the German Allies, that the Reſignation of that Miniſter would not occaſion the leaſt Change in Meaſures, except only that they would be carried on with redoubled Vigour.

THE END.

A LETTER TO THE WORTHY ELECTORS OF THE BOROVGH OF AYLESBVRY, IN THE COVNTY OF BVCKS.

By *JOHN WILKES*, Efq;

LONDON:
Printed for J. ALMON, oppofite Burlington-House, in Piccadilly.

M DCC LXVII.

A LETTER TO THE ELECTORS OF AYLESBURY.

GENTLEMEN,

THE very honourable, unanimous, and repeated marks of esteem, you conferred on me, by committing to my trust your liberty, safety, property, and all those glorious privileges, which are your birth-right as *Englishmen*, entitle you to my warmest thanks and to the highest tribute of gratitude my heart can pay. Yet in the peculiar circumstances of my case, I think that I ought not at present to rest contented with thanking you. I have always found a true plea-

sure

ſure in ſubmitting to you my parliamentary conduct. It is now more particularly my duty, and when I reflect on the real importance and intereſting nature of thoſe great events, in which, as your repreſentative, I have been more immediately concerned, I am exceedingly anxious not barely to juſtify myſelf, but to obtain the ſanction of your approbation. It has ever been my ambition to approve myſelf worthy of the choice you have more than once made of me as your deputy to the great council of the nation, with an unanimity equally honourable and indearing. The conſciouſneſs of having faithfully diſcharged my truſt, of having acted an upright and ſteady part in Parliament, as well as in the moſt arduous circumſtances, makes me dare to hope, that you will continue to me what I moſt value, the good opinion and friendſhip of my worthy conſtituents.

Having the happineſs of being born in the country, where the name of *Vaſſal* is unknown, where *Magna Charta* is the inheritance of the ſubject, I have endeavoured to ſupport and merit thoſe privileges, to which my birth gave me the cleareſt right.

The various charges brought againſt me may be reduced to two heads. The one is of a public, the other of a private nature. The firſt is grounded on the political paper of the *North Briton*, No. 45: the other reſpects a ſmall part of a ludicrous poem, which was ſtolen out of my houſe. The two Accuſations are only ſo far connected, that I am convinced, there is not a man in *England*, who believes, that if the *firſt* had not appeared, the *ſecond* would ever have been called in queſtion. . . . .

The firſt charge is, that *The North Briton*, No 45, is a *falſe Libel*. . .

On my trial before Lord *Mansfield*, the

the word *false* was omitted in the indictment. . . . . .

The word *false* is not to be found among the various epithets applied to this paper in either of the warrants issued by Lord *Halifax*. . . . .

By the first warrant, under which I was apprehended, *The North Briton*, No. 45, was denominated a *treasonable* paper. In the second, by which I was committed to the *Tower*, that word too was omitted, so that the greatest enemies of this paper seem to give up its being either *false* or *treasonable*. . . . It is remarkable, that the epithet *traiterous* is given to *insurrection*, as the *supposed* consequence of a *supposed* libel; whereas the *Scots*, who appeared in open rebellion so lately as 1745, were, in the weekly writings against the *North Briton*, published under the patronage of the *Scottish* Minister, and *paid for by him out of the* —— ——, only termed *in-*

sur-

ſurgents who defeated regular forces. Yet in fact, no *inſurrection of any kind* ever did or could follow from this publication, even in thoſe parts of the kingdom, ſo lately ſubjected to all the inſolence and cruelty of the moſt deſpicable of our ſpecies, the mean petty *Exciſeman.* This is the ſtrongeſt caſe, which can poſſibly be put. The *Exciſe* is the moſt abhorred monſter, which ever ſprung from arbitrary power, and the new mode of it is ſpoken of through this paper as the greateſt grievance on the ſubject; yet *even in this caſe,* obedience to the *laws,* and all *lawful authority,* is ſtrictly enjoined, and no oppoſition, but what is conſiſtent with the *laws* and the *conſtitution,* is allowed. The words are very *temperate, cautious, and well guarded.* "*Every legal Attempt of a contrary tendency to the ſpirit of concord will be deemed a juſtifiable reſiſtance, warranted by the ſpirit of the* English *conſti-*

conſtitution." Is this *withdrawing the people from their obedience to the Laws of the realm? Is reſiſtance* recommended, but expreſſly only ſo far as it is ſtrictly *legal?* Let the impartial public determine, whether this is the language of *ſedition*, or can have the leaſt *tendency* to excite *traiterous inſurrections.*

The general charge that *the North Briton*, No. 45, is a *libel*, ſcarcely deſerves an anſwer, becauſe the term is vague, and ſtill remains undefined by our law. Every man applies it to what he diſlikes. A ſpirited *ſatire* will be deemed a *libel* by a *wicked miniſter*, and by a *corrupt judge*, who feel, or who dread the laſh. . . . . . The *North Briton* did not ſuffer the public to be miſled. He acknowledged no *privileged vehicle of fallacy.* He conſidered the *liberty of the preſs* as the bulwark of all our liberties, as inſtituted to open the eyes of the people; and he he ſeems to have thought it the duty of a political writer to follow *truth* wherever it leads. In his behalf I would aſk even Lord *Manſfield*, Can TRUTH *be a* LIBEL? *Is it ſo in the King's Bench?*

This unlucky paper is likewiſe ſaid,

. . . .

and by the hirelings of the miniſtry it is always in private charged with *perſonal* diſreſpect to the King. It is however, moſt certain, that not a ſingle word *perſonally* diſreſpectful to his Majeſty is to be found in any part of it. On the contrary, the ſovereign is mentioned not only in terms of decency, but with that regard and reverence, which is due from a good ſubject to a good King—*a Prince of ſo many great and amiable qualities, whom* England *truly reveres—the perſonal character of our preſent amiable ſovereign makes us eaſy and happy that ſo great a power is lodged in ſuch hands.* . . .

The author of that paper, ſo far from making any *perſonal* attack on his ſovereign, has even vindicated him *perſonally* from ſome of the late meaſures, which were ſo ſeverely cenſured by the judicious and unbiaſſed public.

He exclaims with an honeſt indignation, *What a ſhame was it to ſee the ſecurity of this country, in point of military force, complimented away,* CONTRARY TO THE OPINION OF ROYALTY ITSELF, *and ſacrificed to the prejudices, and to the ignorance of a ſet of people, the moſt unfit from every conſideration, to be conſulted on a manner relative to the ſecurity of the Houſe of* Hanover? . . The miniſter is indeed every where treated with the contempt and indignation he has merited, but he is ever carefully diſtinguiſhed from the ſovereign. Every kingdom in the world has, in its turn, found occaſion to lament that princes of the

beſt

beſt intentions have been deceived and miſled by wicked and deſigning *miniſters* and *favourites*. It has likewiſe, in moſt countries, been the fate of the new daring patriots, who have honeſtly endeavoured to *undeceive* their ſovereign, to feel the heavieſt marks of his diſpleaſure. It is, however, I think rather wonderful *among us, even in theſe times*, that a paper which contains the moſt dutiful expreſſions of regard to his Majeſty, ſhould be treated with ſuch unuſual ſeverity, and yet that ſo many other publications of the ſame date, full of the moſt deadly venom, ſhould paſs totally unregarded. Some of theſe papers contained the moſt opprobrious reflections on that true patron of liberty, the *late king*, whoſe memory is embalmed with the tears of *Engliſhmen*, while his aſhes are rudely trampled upon by others, whom his godlike attribute of mercy had pardoned the crime of unprovoked rebellion. Others were full of the moſt indecent abuſe on our great proteſtant ally, the King of *Pruſſia*, on the near relation of his preſent Majeſty, who has merited ſo highly of the nation by fixing the crown in the houſe of *Hanover*; on the ſtancheſt friends of freedom, the city of *London*; and on the firſt characters among us. Yet all theſe papers have paſſed uncenſured by miniſters, ſecretaries, and by the two *Houſes of Parliament*. . .

There only remains one other charge, . . .
Under the *arbitrary Stuarts*, when our more than *Roman* ſenates dared to bring *truth* to the foot of the throne, and made the trembling tyrant obey her ſacred voice, the nation was in love with parliaments, becauſe they were the ſteady friends of liberty, and never met but in favour of the

ſubject

ſubject to redreſs real grievances. . .

I have thus, Gentlemen, gone thro' all the objections made againſt this paper . . the treatment I have experienced as the *ſuppoſed* author. . . Orders were given by the deceaſed ſecretary of ſtate, *to drag me out of my bed at midnight*. A good deal of humanity, and ſome ſhare of timidity, prevented the execution of ſuch—— commands. I was made a priſoner in my own houſe by ſeveral of the king's meſſengers, who only produced a *general warrant*, iſſued without oath, neither naming nor deſcribing me. I therefore refuſed to obey a warrant which I knew to be illegal. I was, however, by violence carried before the earls of *Egremont* and *Halifax*, who thought it worth their while to aſk me a tolerable number of plain queſtions, to not one of which I thought it worth my while to give a plain anſwer. It is no ſmall ſatisfaction to me now to know, that I have not a friend in the world who wiſhes a ſingle word *unſaid* by me in the critical moment of that examination. I informed their lordſhips of the orders actually given by the *Court of Common Pleas* for my *Habeas Corpus*, notwithſtanding which I was committed to the *Tower*, the cuſtody of me ſhifted into other hands, and that act for the liberty of the ſubject eluded. Altho' the offence of which I ſtood accuſed was undoubtedly *bailable*, yet for three days every perſon was refuſed admittance to me; and the governor was obliged to treat me in a manner very different from the great humanity of his nature, for he had received orders to conſider me as a *cloſe* priſoner. I rejoice that I can ſay, I am the only inſtance of ſuch rigorous treatment ſince the acceſſion of the mild houſe of *Brunſwick*, although the *Tower* has twice been crowded

crowded even with Rebels from the northern parts of the iſland; and therefore I ſhall continue to regret the . policy . . . . . of conferring on *Scotſmen* ALL the governments of the few conqueſts not tamely given up by the *Scottiſh miniſter*; conqueſts won by the valour of the united forces of *England, Scotland* and *Ireland.* While I ſuffered this harſh confinement, my houſe in *Great George-ſtreet* was plundered, all my papers were ſeized, and ſome of a very *nice* and *delicate* nature, not bearing the moſt diſtant relation to the affairs of government, were divulged. . . . .

When I was brought before the *Common Pleas*, I pleaded the cauſe of *univerſal liberty.* It was not the cauſe of peers and gentlemen only, but of *all the midling and inferior claſs of people, who ſtand moſt in need of protection,* which, I obſerved was on that day the

the great queſtion before the court. I was diſcharged from impriſonment by the unanimous ſentence of my judges, without giving any bail or ſecurity. On the firſt day of the meeting of the parliament, I humbly ſubmitted my grievances to the *Houſe of Commons*, as they were choſen to be the guardians of the liberties of the people againſt the deſpotiſm of miniſters. I likewiſe voluntarily entered my appearance to the actions brought at law againſt me as ſoon as I knew the determination of the *majority*, that all the irregularities againſt me ſhould be juſtified, and that no *privilege* ſhould be allowed *in my caſe*, even as to the mode of proceeding, which was the moſt harſh the rancour of party could deviſe.

. . . .

Plurima deſunt.

. . . .

I now

I now proceed to the other charge brought againſt me, which reſpects an idle poem, called, *An Eſſay on Woman*, and a few other detached verſes. If ſo much had not been ſaid on this ſubject, I ſhould be ſuperior to entering upon any juſtification of myſelf, becauſe I will always maintain the right of private opinion in its full extent, when it is not followed by giving any open public offence to any eſtabliſhment, or indeed to any individual. The crime commences from thence, and the magiſtrate has a right to interpoſe, and even to puniſh outrageous and indecent attacks on what any community has decreed to be ſacred, not only the rules of good breeding, but the laws of ſociety are then infringed. In my own cloſet I had a right to examine, and even to try by the keen edge of ridicule any opinions I pleaſed. If I have laughed pretty freely at the glaring abſurdities of . . .

a creed,

a creed, which our great *Tillotson wished the church of England was fairly rid of*, it was in private I laughed. . . . . . I gave, however, no offence to any one individual of the community. The fact is, that after the affair of the *North Briton*, . . bribed one of my servants to *steal* a part of the *Essay on Woman*, and the other pieces, out of my house. Not quite a *fourth* part of the volume had been printed at my own private press. The work had been discontinued for several months before I had the least knowledge of the theft. Of that *fourth* part only twelve copies were worked off, and I never gave one of those copies to any friend. In this infamous manner did —— get possession of this new subject of accusation, and except in the case of *Algernon Sidney*, of this new species of crime; for a *S*—— only could make the refinement in tyranny of ransack-

ing

ing and robbing the recesses of closets and studies, in order to convert *private amusements into state crimes.* After the servant had been bribed to commit the theft in his master's house, the most abandoned man of the age, ... was bribed to make a complaint . . that I had *published* an infamous *poem*, which no man there had ever seen. It was read before . .

. . . *excellent judges of wit and poetry*, . .

. . . The neat, prim, smirking *chaplain* of that babe of grace, that *gude cheeld* of the prudish *Kirk* of *Scotland*, the . . was highly offended at my having made an *Essay on Woman. His nature* could not forgive me that *ineffable crime*, and *his own conduct* did not afford me the shadow of an apology. In great wrath he drew his grey goose quill against me. The *pious peer* caught the alarm,

larm, and they both pour'd forth, moſt woeful lamentations, their tender hearts overwhelmed with *grief*, or as the *chaplain*, who held the pen, ſaid, with *grief of griefs*. He proceeded to make very unfair extracts, and afterwards to *benote* them in the fouleſt manner. The moſt vile blaſphemies were forged *, and publiſhed as

* "A print, under which is engraved in the Greek language and character, THE SAVIOUR OF THE WORLD." *Kidgell's Narrative.*

Anſwer. What Mr. Kidgell ſays relative to the Greek inſcription, which he tranſlates THE SAVIOUR OF THE WORLD, ſo fully demonſtrates his ignorance of what is blaſphemy, and how much he miſtakes the thing, that though Mr. Wilkes has not thought it worth his while to take the leaſt notice of it, yet I cannot omit ſhewing the reverend gentleman's total want of ſcholarſhip. He ought to have known, that the words ΣΩΤΗΡ ΚΟΣΜΟΥ, which compoſe the Inſcription, have no relation to chriſtianity, and therefore the alluſion is a blaſphemy, and *not* of the Author of the *Eſſay on Woman*. That Inſcrip-

as · part of a work which in reality contained but . . . . . a few portraits drawn warm from life, with the too high colouring of a youthful fancy, and two or three deſcriptions, perhaps · too luſcious, which though *nature* and *woman* might pardon, a Inſcription was found upon an ancient PHALLUS, of a date of much more remote antiquity than the birth of Chriſt. The account of this antique may be ſeen at large in De la Chauſsée's Muſeum Romanum, printed at Rome, in folio, in 1692, and by *his own permiſſion*, dedicated to the Pope, who, I ſuppoſe, is a chriſtian prince.

The late reverend learned Dr. Middleton, in that valuable work, entitled, *Germana quædam Antiquitatis eruditæ Monumenta*, &c. has not ſcrupled to give the following ſhort account of it: "Quod quidem illuſtrari quodammado videtur a "ſymbolica quadam apud cauſæum priapi effigiæ, "cui Galli Gallinacei caput criſta ornatum, roſ- "tri vero loco, faſcinum ingens datur: cujuſque "in baſi litteris Græcis inſcriptum legitur "ΣΩΤΗΡ ΚΟΣΜΟΥ. SERVATOR ORBIS. Quæ "omnia vil doctus ita interpretatur: *Gallum ſcilicet, avem ſoli ſacram eſſe; ſolemque generatricis facultatis præſidem; pudendumque ides verile Gallinaceo capiti adjunctum denotare, quod a conjunctis ſolis priapique viribus, animalium genus omne procreatum et conſervatum ſit, ſecundum phyſicum quoddam Ariſtotelis axicma,* Homo hominem generat et ſol.

Kidgel and a —— could not fail to condemn.

I have now, gentlemen, gone thro' all the objections which have been made to my conduct in a *public* capacity. My enemies finding that I was invulnerable, where they pointed their most envenomed darts, afterwards attempted to assassinate my private character, and propagated an infinite variety of groundless calumnies against me. I have generally treated these with the contempt they deserved, from the certainty that all who knew me would know that I was incapable of the things laid to my charge. A few falshoods, advanced with more boldness than the rest, I was at the pains to refute. The *Winchester* story in particular, because it respected Lord *Bute*'s own son, and had been ushered to the public with the greatest parade, as well as with all the impudence of malice, and rage of party, I disproved

ved ſo fully, that I am ſure not the leaſt ſhadow of a doubt remained in any man's mind as to my entire innocence of that moſt illiberal charge. I have lived ſo long among you, gentlemen, that I will reſt every thing reſpecting me as a private man to the teſtimony, which the experience of ſo many years authorizes you to give, well knowing, that true candour always weighs in the ſame balance, faults and virtues. The ſhades in private life are darkened by an enemy, but ſcarcely ſeen by a friend. Beſides, it is not given to every man to be as *pious* as lord ——, or as *chaſte* in and out of the marriage bed, in all thought, word, and deed, as the —.

A few other particulars, gentlemen, deſerve to be mentioned, that you may have before you the whole of my conduct in theſe intereſting affairs. Immediately after the laſt fragrant breach of the laws, I thought it my duty to the community to commence actions againſt all the perſons guilty. I deſpiſed the meanneſs of attacking only agents and deputies. I endeavoured to bring to the juriſdiction of the law *the principals* —, *the two ſecretaries of State*. I bluſh for my country when I add, that though I have employed the ableſt gentlemen of that profeſſion, they have hitherto found it impoſſible even to force an appearance. Lord *Egremont* died—. Lord *Halifax* lives; . . . The judicial proceeding at my ſuit, commenced at the beginning of *May* twelvemonth, and now in the end of *October* in the preſent year, his lordſhip has not entered any appearance, . . . The *little offenders* indeed have not eſcaped. Several *honeſt juries* have marked them with ignominy, and their guilt has been followed with legal puniſhment. But what is of infinitely greater importance

tance to the nation, we have heard from the bench, that *general warrants are absolutely illegal.* Such a declaration is in the highest degree interesting to the subject.

When I reflect on these two most important determinations in favour of *Liberty*, the best cause and the noblest stake for which men can contend, I congratulate my free-born countrymen, and am full of gratitude that Heaven inspired me with a firmness and fortitude equal to the conduct of so arduous a business. . . The goodness of the cause supported me, and I never lost sight of the great object which I had from the first in my view, the preservation of the rights and privileges of *Englishmen.* I glory in the name, and will never forget the duties resulting from it. Though I am driven into exile from my dear country, I shall never cease to love and reverence its constitution, while it remains free. It will continue my first ambition to approve myself a faithful son of *England*; and I shall always be ready to give my life a willing sacrifice to my native country, and to what it holds most dear, the security of our invaluable liberties. While I live, I shall enjoy the satisfaction of thinking that I have not lived in vain; that the present age has borne the noblest testimony to me, and that my name will pass with honour to posterity, for the upright and disinterested part I have acted, and for my unwearied endeavours *to protect and secure the persons, houses, and papers of my fellow subjects from arbitrary visits and seizures.*

I am, GENTLEMEN,

With much regard and affection,

Your most obliged,

And obedient humble servant,

Paris, Oct. 22, 1764.

JOHN WILKES.

BOOKS *Printed for* J. ALMON, *opposite* Burlington House, *in* Piccadilly.

In January next will be published,

VOLUME the FIRST, of

THE HISTORY of ENGLAND, From the REVOLUTION, to the End of the 4th year of K. GEORGE the Third.

By JOHN WILKES, Esq;

"Nimium TARQUINOS regno assuesse—non pla-
"cere nomen, periculosum LIBERTATI esse.

LIVY.

"Ego hoc laboris præmium peto, uti me à con-
"spectu malorum, quæ nostra quatuor pœnè
"per annos vidit ætas, tantisper certè, dum
"prisca illa totâ mente repeto, avertam, om-
"nis expers curæ, quæ scribentis aninum,
"estí non flectere à vero, solicitum, tamen ef-
"ficere possit."

Ibid.

*** This Work will make three volumes in quarto. The first contains the reigns of King William and Queen Anne; and is compiled from a variety of interesting Materials, which no other Historian has seen.

I. The POLITICAL REGISTER, and IMPARTIAL REVIEW OF NEW BOOKS. Published monthly. Price one Shilling each Number, the first of which came out June 1, 1767. This work is divided into two parts; the first consists wholly of original essays and interesting papers, many of them written and communicated by persons of emi-

nence;

nence; and the other a candid and disinterested account of all new Publications.

II. The SPEECHES, ARGUMENTS, and DETERMINATIONS of the Right Hon. the Lords of Council and Session in Scotland, upon that important Cause, wherein his Grace the Duke of Hamilton, and Others, were Plaintiffs, and Archibald Douglass, of Douglass, Esq; Defendant. Together with an introductory Preface, giving an impartial and distinct account of this Suit.

By a BARRISTER at LAW.

As this Cause hath made a great noise all over Europe, the Public will doubtless be curious to see the particulars of so solemn a decree; and these they may be assured, as herein related, are perfectly genuine and correct.

III. A complete Collection of the LORDS PROTESTS. From the first upon record, in the reign of Henry III. to the present time. In two vols. 8vo. Pr. 12 s. bound.

The first collection of Protests was published in 1735, the second in 1743, and the third in 1747, all of them beginning with the year 1641, and ending with the dates of their respective publications. The collection which is here offered to the public, ascends

aſcends to the firſt upon record in 1242, and is continued to the end of June 1767, thereby including many not made public before, and particularly ſeveral during the laſt twenty years; which will, in all probability, be eſteemed the moſt intereſting, as the ſubjects, which gave occaſion to them, are allowed to be of the utmoſt importance. This Work is accompanied with an accurate and copious Index, which the other collections want.

And to the whole is ſubjoined, an hiſtorical Eſſay on the legiſlative power of England; wherein the origin of both Houſes of Parliament, their ancient Conſtitution, and the changes that have happened in the perſons that compoſed them, are related in chronological order.

IV. A new and impartial Collection of Intereſting LETTERS, from the public papers; many of them written by perſons of eminence, on a great variety of important ſubjects, which have occaſionally engaged the public attention; from the acceſſion of his preſent Majeſty in Oct. 1760, to May 1767. In two vols. 8vo. price 10s. bound.

The merit and importance which the news-papers have, of late years, acquired from the liberal communications of gen-

tlemen

tlemen of the first rank, both in politicks and literature, have excited an universal regret, at seeing the valuable productions of such writers doomed indiscriminately to oblivion with the fugitive pieces of the day. —It was the want of a proper publication wherein to distinguish the writings of such authors, that suggested the idea of this Collection, the intention of which is to preserve and transmit to posterity, such sensible and well-written papers as appeared during the years 1760, 1761, 1762, 1763, 1764, 1765, 1766, and 1767, on both sides of every question which arose from the circumstances of the times, the necessities of the state, or the humour of the age.

V. The HISTORY of the MINORITY, during the years 1762, 1763, 1764, and 1765. Exhibiting the conduct, principles, and views of that party. A new edition, being the fourth, with several additions. Price 5s. bound, or 4s. sewed.

*** The very extraordinary, and almost singular success which this book hath met with, is the strongest and best testimony of its merit. It has moreover been translated in Holland, France, and other foreign nations; in which as well as in England, it is much read and esteemed.

A LETTER TO HIS GRACE THE DVKE OF GRAFTON, FIRST COMMISSIONER OF HIS MAJESTY's TREASVRY.

Vacare culpâ magnum est solatium; præsertim cum habeam duas res quibus me sustentem, optimarum artium scientiam, et maximarum rerum gloriam, quarum altera mihi vivo nunquam eripietur, altera ne mortuo quidem.

Cicero.

THE EIGHTH EDITION.

LONDON:

Printed for J. ALMON, opposite *Burlington-House, Piccadilly*. MDCCLXVII.

Paris, Dec. 12. 1766.

MY LORD,

I AM not yet recovered from the aſtoniſhment, into which I was thrown by your grace's *verbal* meſſage, in anſwer to my letter of the firſt of November. In a converſation I had with colonel *Fitzroy* at the hotel d'*Eſpagne*, he did me the honour of aſſuring me, that I ſhould find his brother my real and ſincere friend, extremely deſirous to concur in doing me juſtice, that he was to tell me this from your grace, but that many intereſting particulars relative to me could not be communicated by letter, nor by the poſt. I fondly believed theſe obliging aſſurances, becauſe on a variety of occaſions your grace had teſtified a full approbation of my conduct, had thanked me in the moſt flattering terms, as the perſon the moſt uſeful to the common cauſe in which we were embarked, and had ſhewn an uncommon zeal to ſerve a man who had ſuffered ſo much in the cauſe of liberty.

I returned to *England* with the gayeſt, and the moſt lively hopes. As ſoon as I arrived at London, I deſired my excellent friend, Mr. *Fitzherbert*, to wait on your grace, with every profeſſion of regard on my part, and the reſolution I had taken of entirely ſubmitting the mode of the application I ſhould make to the throne for my pardon. I cannot expreſs the anxiety, which your grace's anſwer gave me, *Mr. Wilkes muſt write to lord Chatham.* I then begged Mr. *Fitzherbert* to ſtate the reaſons, which made it impoſſible for me to follow that advice, from every principle of honour, both public and private. I ſhewed too the impropriety of ſupplicating a fellow ſubject for mercy, the *prerogative* good Kings are the moſt jealous of, by far the brighteſt jewel in their crown, and the attribute, by which they may the neareſt approach to the Divinity.

I afterwards wrote the letter * to your grace, which I have ſeen in all

* *That Letter was as follows.*

My Lord,

IT is a very peculiar ſatisfaction I feel, on my

the public prints. I never received any other anſwer but a *verbal* meſſage,

return to my native country, that a nobleman of your grace's ſuperior talents, and inflexible integrity, is at the head of the moſt important department of ſtate. I have been witneſs of the general applauſe, which has been given abroad, to the choice his majeſty has made, and I am happy to find my own countrymen zealous and unanimous in every teſtimony of their approbation.

I hope, my Lord, that I may congratulate myſelf, as well as my country, on your grace's being placed in a ſtation of ſo great power and importance. Though I have been cut off from the body of his majeſty's ſubjects, by a cruel and unjuſt proſcription, I have never entertained an idea inconſiſtent with the duty of a good ſubject. My heart ſtill retains all its former warmth for the dignity of England, and the glory of its ſovereign. I have not aſſociated with the traitors to our liberties, nor made a ſingle connection with any man who was dangerous, or even ſuſpected by the friends of the proteſtant family on the throne. I now hope that the rigour of a long-unmerited exile is paſt, and that I may be allowed

Mr. Wilkes muſt write to lord Chatham: I do nothing without lord Chatham.

to continue in the land and among the friends of liberty.

I wiſh, my lord, to owe this to the mercy of my prince. I entreat your grace to lay me with all humility at the king's feet, with the trueſt aſſurances, that I have never, in any moment of my life, ſwerved from the duty and allegiance I owe to my ſovereign, and that I implore, and in every thing ſubmit to, his majeſty's clemency.

Your grace's noble manner of thinking, and the obligations I have formerly received, which are ſtill freſh in my mind, will, I hope, give a full propriety to this addreſs; and I am ſure a heart, glowing with the ſacred zeal of liberty, muſt have a favourable reception from the duke of *G----*. I flatter myſelf, that my conduct will juſtify your grace's interceding with a prince, who is diſtinguiſhed by a compaſſionate tenderneſs and goodneſs to all his ſubjects.

I am, with the trueſt reſpect, My Lord,
Your Grace's moſt obedient, and moſt humble ſervant,
JOHN WILKES.

When I found that my pardon was to be bought with the ſacrifice of my honour, I had the virtue not to heſitate. I ſpurned at the propoſal, and left my dear native London with a heart full of grief, that my faireſt hopes were blaſted, of humiliation, that I had given an eaſy faith to the promiſes of a miniſter and a courtier, and of aſtoniſhment that a nobleman of parts and diſcernment could continue in an infatuation, from which the conduct of *lord Chatham* had recovered every other man in the nation. He was indeed long the favourite character of our countrymen. Every tongue was wanton in his praiſe. The whole people laviſhed on him their choiceſt favours, and endeavoured by the nobleſt means, by an unbounded generosity and confidence, to have kept him virtuous. With what anguish were we at last undeceived! How much it cost us to give up a man, who had so long entirely kept possession of our hearts! How cruel was the struggle! But alas! how is he changed? how fallen? from what height fallen? His glorious sun is set, I believe never to rise again.

We long hoped, my lord, that public virtue was the *guide* of his actions, and the love of our country his ruling passion, but he has fully shewn *omnis vis virtusque in linguâ sita est*. Our hearts glowed with gratitude for the important services he had done against the common enemy, and the voice of the nation hailed him our deliverer; but private ambition was all the while ſkulking behind the ſhield of the patriot, and at length in an evil hour made him quit the ſcene of all his glory, the only place, in which he could be truly uſeful, for a retreat, where he knew it was impoſſible the confidence of the people could follow, but where he might in inglorious eaſe bear his BLUSHING *honours thick upon him.*

I might now, my lord, expoſtulate with your grace on a *verbal* meſſage, and of ſuch a nature, in anſwer to a letter couched in the moſt decent and reſpectful terms, coming too from a late member of the legiſlature. I might regret, that the largeſt proffers of friendſhip, and real ſervice, could mean no more than two or three words of cold advice, that I ſhould apply to another. I might be tempted to think it a duty of office in the firſt lord of the treaſury to have ſubmitted to his majeſty a petition relative to the exerciſe of the nobleſt act of regal power, which any conſtitution can give any ſovereign. Surely, my lord, my application to the firſt commiſſioner of the treaſury, who is always conſidered as the firſt miniſter in England, was the very proper application. As I had made no diſcovery of any new wonderful pill or drop, nor pretended to the ſecret of curing the gout or the tooth-ach, I never thought of ſoliciting *Lord Chatham for a privy ſeal.* His lordſhip's office was neither important, nor reſponſible. I will not however enlarge on this, but I ſhall deſire your grace's permiſſion fully to ſtate what has happened to me as a private gentleman relative to *lord Chatham*, becauſe I would not leave a doubt concerning the propriety of my conduct, in a mind naturally ſo candid, and ſo capable of judging truly, as that of the *duke of Grafton*.

I believe that the flinty heart of L— C—— has known the ſweets of private friendſhip, and the fine feelings of humanity, as little as even —— ———. They are both formed to be admired, not beloved. A proud, inſolent, overbearing, ambitious man, is always full of the ideas of his own importance, and vainly imagines himſelf ſuperior to the equality neceſſary among real friends, in all the moments of true enjoyment. Friendſhip is too pure a pleaſure for a mind cankered with ambition, or the luſt of power and grandeur. *Lord Chatham* declared in parliament the ſtrongeſt attachment to *lord Temple*, one of the greateſt characters our country could ever boaſt, and ſaid, *he would live and die with his noble brother.* He has received obligations of the firſt magnitude from that *noble brother*, yet what trace of gratitude or of friendſhip was ever found in any part of his conduct? And has he not now declared the moſt open variance, and even hoſtility? I have had as warm and expreſs declarations of regard as could be made by this marble-hearted friend, and *Mr. Pitt* had no doubt his views in even feeding me with flattery from time to time; on occaſions too where candour and indulgence were all I could claim. He may remember the compliments he paid me on two certain poems in the year 1754. If I were to take the declarations made by himſelf and the late *Mr. Potter à la lettre*, they were more charmed with thoſe verſes after the ninety-ninth reading than after the firſt; ſo that from this circumſtance, as well as a few of his ſpeeches in parliament, it ſeems to be likewiſe true of the firſt orator, or rather the firſt comedian, of our age, *non diſplicuiſſe illi jocos, ſed non contigiſſe.*

I will now ſubmit to your grace, if there was not ſomething peculiarly baſe and perfidious in *Mr.* —'s calling me a *blaſphemer of my God* for thoſe very verſes, at a time when I was abſent, and dangerouſly ill from an affair of honour. The charge too he knew was falſe, for the whole ridicule of thoſe two pieces was confined to certain myſteries, which formerly the *unplaced and unpenſioned Mr. P--* did not think himſelf obliged even to affect to believe. He added another charge equally unjuſt, that I was the *libeller of my king*, though he was ſenſible that I never wrote a ſingle line diſreſpectful to the ſacred perſon of my ſovereign, but had only attacked the deſpotiſm of his miniſters, with the ſpirit becoming a good ſubject, and zealous friend of his country. The reaſon of this perfidy was plain. He was then beginning to pay homage to the *Scottiſh* Idol, and I was the moſt acceptable ſacrifice he could offer at the ſhrine of BUTE. Hiſtory ſcarcely gives ſo remarkable a change. He was a few years ago the mad, ſeditious tribune of the people, inſulting his ſovereign even in his capital city, now he is the abject, crouching deputy of the proud Scot, who he declared in parliament *wanted wiſdom, and held principles incompatible with freedom*; a moſt ridiculous character ſurely for a ſtateſman, and the ſubject of a free kingdom, but the very proper compoſition for a *favourite*. Was it poſſible for me after this to write a ſuppliant letter to *L— Ch——*? I am the firſt to pronounce myſelf moſt unworthy of a pardon, if I could have obtained it on thoſe terms.

Although I declare, my lord, that the conſcious pride of virtue makes me look down with contempt on a man, who could be guilty of this baſeneſs, who could in the lobby declare that I muſt be ſupported, and in the houſe on the ſame day deſert and revile me, yet I will on every occaſion do juſtice to the miniſter. He has ſerved the public in all thoſe points, where the good of the nation coincided with his own private views; and in no other. I venerate the memory of the ſecretary, and I think it an honour to myſelf that I ſteadily ſupported in parliament an adminiſtration, the moſt ſucceſsful we ever had, and which carried the glory of the nation to the higheſt pitch in every part of the world. He found his country almoſt in deſpair. He raiſed the noble ſpirit of England, and ſtrained every nerve againſt our enemies. His plans, when in power, were always great, though in direct oppoſition to the declarations of his whole life, when out of power. The invincible bravery of the British troops gave success even to the most rash, the most extravagant, the most desperate of his projects. He saw early the hostile intentions of Spain, and if the *written advice* had been followed, a very few weeks had then probably closed the last general war; although the merit of that *advice* was more the merit of his *noble brother*, than his own. After the omnipotence of lord Bute in 1761 had forced Mr. Pitt to retire from his majesty's councils, and the cause was declared by himself to be our conduct relative to Spain, I had the happiness of setting that affair in so clear and advantageous a light, that he expressed the most entire satisfaction, and particular obligations to my friendship. I do not however make this a claim of merit to Mr. Pitt. It was my duty, from the peculiar advantages of information I then had.

The conſtitution of our country has no obligations to him. He has left it with all its beauties, and all its blemiſhes. He never once appeared in earneſt about any queſtion of liberty. He was the cauſe that in 1764 no point was gained for the public in the two great queſtions of GENERAL WARRANTS, and the SEIZURE OF PAPERS. The curſed remains of the court of Star-chamber, the enormous power of the attorney-general, the ſole great judicial officer of the crown, who is *durante bene placito*, and not upon oath, who tramples on *grand juries*, and breaks down the firſt, the foremoſt barriers of liberty, continued during his adminiſtration the ſame as before. Every grievance, which was not rooted out by the glorious revolution, and the latter ſtruggles of our patriots, ſtill ſubſiſts in full force, notwithſtanding the abſolute power he exerciſed for ſeveral years over every department of the ſtate. But I have done with *L—C——*. I leave him to the poor conſolation of a place, a penſion, and a peerage, for which he has ſold the confidence of a great nation. Pity ſhall find and weep over him.

I am now, my lord, once more driven from the *Romans*, to the gay, the polite *Athenians*, but I ſhall endeavour to convince your grace that I am not totally loſt to my country nor to myſelf, in this ſcene of elegant diſſipation, and that I do not waſte the time in unavailing complaints of my hard fate, and the ingratitude of thoſe I have ſerved with ſucceſs, for I ſhall very ſoon beg to call the public attention to ſome points of national importance, and in the mean time I ſhall embrace this opportunity of doing myſelf juſtice againſt the calumnies, which a reſtleſs faction does not ceaſe to propagate.

The affair of the GENERAL WARRANT, and the HABEAS CORPUS, is told very unfaithfully, and almoſt every particular, relative to my being made a priſoner, and ſent to the Tower on the 30th of April 1763, has been injuriouſly miſrepreſented in ſeveral late publications. I ſhall therefore ſtate the tranſactions of that memorable day, and I may appeal to the minutes taken at the time for the accuracy of this relation.

On my return from the city early in the morning, I met at the end of Great George-ſtreet one of the king's meſſengers. He told me that he had a *warrant* to apprehend me, which he muſt execute immediately, and that I muſt attend him to lord Halifax's. I deſired to ſee the *warrant*. He ſaid it was *againſt the authors, printers, and publiſhers of the North-Briton*, No. 45, and that his verbal orders were to arreſt *Mr. Wilkes*. I told him the *warrant* did not reſpect me: I adviſed him to be very civil, and to uſe no violence in the ſtreet, for if he attempted force, I would put him to death in the inſtant, but if he would come quietly to my houſe, I would convince him of the illegality of the *warrant*, and the injuſtice of the orders he had received. He choſe to accompany me home, and then produced the *GENERAL WARRANT*. I declared that ſuch a *warrant* was abſolutely illegal and void in itſelf, that it was a ridiculous *warrant* againſt the whole Engliſh nation, and I aſked why he would ſerve it on me, rather than on the lord chancellor, on either of the ſecretaries, on lord Bute, or lord Corke, my next door neighbour. The anſwer was, *I am to arreſt Mr. Wilkes.* About an hour afterwards two other meſſengers arrived, and ſeveral of their aſſiſtants. They all endeavoured in vain to perſuade me to accompany them to lord Halifax's. I had likewiſe many civil meſſages from his lordſhip to deſire my attendance. My only anſwer was, that I had not the honour of viſiting his lordſhip, and this firſt application was rather rude and ungentleman-like.

While ſome of the meſſengers and their aſſiſtants were with me, *Mr. Churchill* came into the room. I had heard that their *verbal* orders were likewiſe to apprehend him, but I ſuſpected they did not know his perſon, and by preſence of mind I had the happineſs of ſaving my friend. As ſoon as Mr. *Churchill* entered the room, I accoſted him, *Good morrow, Mr. Thomſon. How does Mrs. Thomſon do to-day? Does ſhe dine in the country? Mr. Churchill* thanked me, ſaid ſhe then waited for him, that he only came for a moment to aſk me how I did, and almoſt directly took his leave. He went home immediately, ſecured all his papers, and retired into the country. The meſſengers could never get intelligence where he was. The following week he came to town, and was preſent both the days of hearing at the court of Common Pleas.

The whole morning paſſed in meſſages between lord Halifax and me. The buſineſs of the meſſengers being ſoon publickly known, ſeveral of my friends came to me on ſo extraordinary an event. I deſired two or three of them to go to the court of COMMON PLEAS, to make affidavit of my being made a priſoner in my own houſe under an illegal *warrant*, and to demand a HABEAS CORPUS. The chief Juſtice gave orders that it ſhould iſſue immediately.

A conſtable came afterwards with ſeveral aſſiſtants to the meſſengers. I repeatedly inſiſted on their all leaving me, and declared I would not ſuffer any one of them to continue in the room againſt my conſent, for I knew and would ſupport the rights of an Engliſhman in the ſanctuary of his own houſe. I was then threatened with immediate violence, and a regiment of the guards, if neceſſary. I ſoon found all reſiſtance would be vain. The conſtable demanded my ſword, and inſiſted on my immediately attending the meſſengers to lord Halifax's. I replied, that if they were not aſſaſſins, they ſhould firſt give me their names in writing. They complied with this, and thirteen ſet their hands to the paper. I then got into my own chair, and proceeded to lord Halifax's, guarded by the meſſengers and their aſſiſtants.

I was conducted into a great apartment fronting the park, where lord Halifax and lord Egremont, the two ſecretaries of ſtate, were ſitting at a table covered with paper, pens and ink. The under-ſecretaries ſtood near their lordſhips. Mr. Lovel Stanhope the law clerk, and Mr. Philip Carteret Webb, the ſolicitor of the treaſury, were the only perſons beſides who attended. Lord Egremont received me with a ſupercilious, inſolent air; lord Halifax with great politeneſs. I was deſired to take the chair near their lordſhips, which I did. Lord

Halifax then began, *that he was really concerned that he had been necessitated to proceed in that manner against me, that it was exceedingly to be regretted that a gentleman of my rank and abilities could engage against his king and his majesty's government.* I replied, *that his lordship could not be more mistaken, for the king had not a subject more zealously attached to his person and government than myself, that I had all my life been a warm friend of the house of Brunswick, and the protestant succession, that while I made the truest professions of duty to the king, I was equally free to declare in the same moment, that I believed no prince had ever the misfortune of being served by such ignorant, insolent, and despotic ministers, of which my being there was a fresh, glaring proof, for I was brought before their lordships by force, under a* GENERAL WARRANT, *which named no body, in violation of the laws of my country, and of the privileges of parliament; that I beg'd both their lordships to remember my present declaration, that on the very first day of the ensuing session of parliament, I would stand up in my place and impeach them for the outrage they had committed in my person against the liberties of the people.* Lord Halifax answered, *that nothing had been done but by the advice of the best lawyers, and that it was now his duty to examine me.* He had in his hand a long list of questions, regularly numbered. He began, *Mr Wilkes do you know Mr. Kearsly? when did you see him? &c. &c.* I replied, *that I suspected there was a vain hope my answer would tend rather to what his lordship wished to know, that he seemed to be loſt in a dark, and intricate path, and really wanted much light to guide him thro' it, but that I could aſſure his lordſhip not a ſingle ray ſhould come from me.* Lord Halifax returned to the charge, *Mr Wilkes do you know Mr Kearſly? &c. &c.* I ſaid, *that this was a curioſity on his lordſhip's part, which however laudable in the ſecretary, I did not find myſelf diſpoſed to gratify, and that at the end of my examination all the quires of paper on their lordſhips' table ſhould be as milk white as at the beginning.* Lord Halifax then *deſired to remind me of my being their priſoner, and of their right to examine me.* I anſwered, *that I ſhould imagine their lordſhips' time was too precious to be trifled away in that manner, that they might have ſeen before I would never ſay one word they deſired to know,* and

I added, *Indeed, my lords, I am not made of ſuch ſlight, flimſy ſtuff*; then, turning to lord Egremont, I ſaid, *could you employ tortures, I would never utter a word unbecoming my honour, or affecting the ſacred confidence of any friend. God has given me firmneſs and fidelity. You trifle away your time moſt egregiouſly, my lords.* Lord Halifax then adviſed me, *to weigh well the conſequences of my conduct, and the advantages to myſelf of a generous, frank confeſſion, I lamented the proſtitution of the word,* GENEROUS, *to what I ſhould conſider as an act of the utmoſt treachery, cowardice and wickedneſs.* His lordſhip then aſked me, *if I choſe to be priſoner in my own houſe, at the Tower, or in Newgate, for he was diſpoſed to oblige me.* I gave his lordſhip my thanks, but, *I deſired to remark, that*

I never received an obligation, but from a friend, that I demanded justice, and my immediate liberty, as an englishman, who had not offended the laws of his country; that as to the rest, it was beneath my attention, the odious idea of restraint was the same odious idea every where; that I would go where I pleased, and if I was restrained by a superior force, I must yield to the violence, but would never give colour to it by a shameful compromise; that every thing was indifferent to me in comparison of my honour and liberty; that I made my appeal to the laws; and had already by my friends applied to the COURT OF COMMON PLEAS *for the* HABEAS CORPUS, *which the chief Justice had actually ordered to be issued, and that I hoped to owe my discharge solely to my innocence, and to the vigour of the law in a free country*. Lord Halifax then told me, *that I ſhould be ſent to the Tower, where I ſhould be treated in a manner ſuitable to my rank*, and that he *hoped the meſſengers had behaved well to me*. I acknowledged that they had *behaved with humanity, and even civility to me, notwithſtanding the ruffian orders given them by his lordſhip's colleague*. I then turned again to lord Egremont, and ſaid, *Your lordſhip's verbal orders were to drag me out of my bed at midnight. The firſt man, who had entered my bed chamber by force, I ſhould have laid dead on the ſpot. Probably I ſhould have fallen in the ſkirmiſh with the others. I thank God, not your lordſhip, that ſuch a ſcene of blood has been avoided. Your lordſhip is very ready to iſſue orders, which you have neither courage to ſign, nor I believe to juſtify.*

No reply was made to this. The conversation dropped. Lord Halifax retired into another apartment. Lord Egremont continued ſullen and ſilent about a quarter of an hour. I then made a few remarks on ſome capital pictures, which were in the room, and his lordſhip left me alone.

I was afterwards conducted into another apartment. I found there ſeveral of my friends, in argument with the moſt infamous of all the tools of that adminiſtration *Mr. P—C—— —.* He confirmed to me, that I was to be carried to the Tower, and *wiſhed to know if I had any favours to aſk.* I replied, *that I was uſed to confer, not to receive favours, that I was ſuperior to the receiving any even from his Maſters, that all I would ſay to him was, if my valet de chambre was allowed to attend me in the Tower, I ſhould be ſhaved and have a clean ſhirt, if he was not, I ſhould have a long beard, and dirty linnen.* Mr. W— ſaid, *that orders would be given for his admiſſion at the Tower.* I complained of the ſhameful evaſion of the *Habeas Corpus* in ſending me to the Tower, though the orders of the *chief juſtice Pratt* were known. Mr W— made no reply to this. He came to viſit me at the Tower in the beginning of my impriſonment, when I had not the permiſſion to ſee any friend. I deſired him almoſt at his firſt entrance to take his leave *for if I was not allowed to ſee thoſe I loved, I would not ſee thoſe I deſpiſed.*

While I continued in the Tower, I was preſſed to offer bail in order to regain my liberty, and two of the firſt nobility deſired to be my ſecurities in the ſum of £. 100,000 each. I was exceedingly grateful for the offer, but would not accept it. I obſerved, that neither my health nor my ſpirits were affected, that I would by great temperance and abſtinence endeavour to compenſate the want of air and exerciſe, but if my health ſuffered in a dangerous way, I would then accept ſuch generous offers, for I hoped to live that ſo noble a cauſe might be brought to a glorious iſſue for the liberties of my country. From the beginning of this arduous buſineſs, I would not on any occaſion give bail, by which I never involved any friend, and remained the perfect maſter of my own conduct.

I ſhall now, my lord, proceed to do myſelf juſtice againſt a calumny of ——— ———, a p-rſ-n of the meaneſt natural parts, and infinitely beneath all regard, except from the —— he bears, with the utmoſt diſcredit to himſelf, with equal diſgrace and inſufficiency to the public. I find the —— acquainted, that —, upon Tueſday laſt, received a letter by the general poſt from Mr. W——, dated Paris the 11th inſtant, incloſing a paper in the French Language, purporting to be a Certificate of one of the French king's phyſicians, and of a ſurgeon of the ſaid king's army, relating to the ſtate of Mr. Wilkes's health, ſubſcribed with two names, but not authenticated before a notary public, nor the ſignature thereof verified in any manner whatſoever. Then follow the *letter* and *certificate*. The inſinuation is too plain to be overlooked. The ſignature was verified by my letter. It is certain that the certificate was in all the uſual forms; yet tho' the affair was determined with reſpect to me, and I was expelled the —— on the ſame day, without any time being allowed for other proof, a regard to truth, and my own honour, made me give the moſt compleat anſwer to this. I ſent a ſecond certificate in the form they had preſcribed themſelves, atteſted by two notaries, and confirmed by the Engliſh E———. I wrote likewiſe again to ——— on the 5th of February following, but neither the ſecond letter, certificate, or atteſtation, is to be found in the ——. I have, however, my lord, taken care that they ſhould be publiſhed, for in a free government like ours, I will endeavour through my life to emulate the ſpirit of ancient Rome, *provoco ad populum*; and while the people do not condemn me, I ſhall, perhaps in this, moſt certainly in every ſucceeding age, riſe ſuperior to any party cabal, or court faction. This ſtep covered my enemies with confuſion, but was of no farther ſervice to me. The party war againſt me ceaſed of courſe in ——, but flamed with equal fury in ——.

By the ——, page 723, I find that I am *guilty of writing and publiſhing the paper, intituled* "The North-Briton, No. 45," and that ſeveral witneſſes were examined. There is not however in the —— a ſingle word of the evidence they gave, and it is well known that not one of them did, or could ſay any thing relative to the *authorſhip*. The evidence of the publication was exceeding ſlight, but the willingneſs of the j— made ample amends for the deficiency of the witneſſes, who were not upon oath. The adminiſtration did not chuſe to riſk either of theſe charges againſt me even in the court of Kings-Bench, and I was only tried for a *re-publication*. I will never bluſh at the imputation of being the *author* of that paper, becauſe I know that truth is reſpected in every line. One circumſtance will ſoon fully appear to the indignant public; I mean the large debt on the civil liſt, contracted chiefly by the ſcandalous purchaſe of a ———— approbation of the late ignominious *peace*, the arbitrary *exciſe*, and other ruinous meaſures of the *Scottiſh* miniſter. But I leave the affair of the *civil liſt* to a future exact diſcuſſion.

The laſt calumny, my lord, which I ſhall diſprove, reſpects the actions at law againſt lord Halifax. It is ſaid that I have neglected, or purpoſely diſcontinued them, ſince my exile. The imputation is totally groundleſs. I was ſo ill at Paris in the beginning of the year 1764, that it was impoſſible for me then to return to England alive, but I gave the moſt expreſs orders that the law proceedings ſhould be carried on with vigour, and in fact there was not a moment's delay. When my wound began to heal in the ſpring, I was diſſuaded by all my friends from returning to a country, where the ſame adminiſtration, which had illegally ſeized my perſon, plundered my houſe, and corrupted the fidelity of my ſervants, were ſtill in full power. I yielded to theſe reaſons, becauſe *propter eorum ſcelus, nihil mihi intra meos parietes tutum, nihil inſidiis vacuum viderem.* Lord Halifax for near two years availed himſelf of every advantage, which privilege and the chicane of law could furniſh. He never entered any appearance to a court of juſtice, and the Common Pleas had, as far as they could, puniſhed ſuch an open contempt, ſuch a daring proof that *Adminiſtration* would not ſubmit to the *law of the land*, and had endeavoured to compel his lordſhip to appear. Towards the end of 1764 I was *outlaw'd.* The proceedings continued againſt his lordſhip till that hour. He then appeared, and his ſingle plea was, that as an *outlaw*, I could not hold any action. No other defence was made againſt the heinous charge of having in my perſon violated the rights of the people.

I felt this, my lord, as the moſt cruel ſtroke, which fortune had given me. Juſtice had at length overtaken many of the inferior criminals, but my *out-lawry* prevented my puniſhing, the great, the capital offender, when after all his ſubterfuges, he was almoſt within my reach. I pleaſe myſelf however with the reflection that no miniſter has ſince dared to iſſue a GENERAL WARRANT, nor to ſign an order for the SEIZURE OF

PAPERS. In the one the perſonal liberty of every ſubject is immediately concerned. On the other may depend not only his own ſafety and property, but what will come ſtill more home to a man of honour, the ſecurity, the happineſs of thoſe, with whom he is moſt intimately connected, their fortunes, their future views, perhaps ſecrets, the diſcovery of which would drive the coldeſt ſtoic to deſpair, their very exiſtence poſſibly, all that is important in the public walk of life, all that is dear and ſacred in friendſhip and in love. I was the *laſt* oppreſſed, but I was the *firſt* man, who had the courage to carry through a juſt reſiſtance to theſe acts of deſpotiſm. Now the opinions of our ſovereign courts of juſtice are known and eſtabliſhed. I rejoice that ſeveral others, who ſuffered before me, have ſince made their appeal to the laws, and obtained redreſs. I hope the iron rod of miniſterial oppreſſion is at length broken, and that I am the laſt victim of violence and cruelty. I ſhall not then regret all the ſacrifices I have made, and my mind ſhall feaſt itſelf with the recollection in the unjuſt exile I am doom'd to ſuffer from my friends and my native land.

I will now, my lord, only add, however unfaſhionable ſuch a declaration may be, that conſiſtency ſhall never depart from my character, that to the laſt moment I will preſerve the ſame fixed and unconquerable hatred to the enemies of freedom and the conſtitution of our happy iſland, the ſame warm attachment to the friends and the cause of liberty, that I keep a ſteady and a longing eye on England, that my endeavours for the good and ſervice of my country, by every method left me, ſhall have a period only with my life, and that although I do not mean to lay any future claim to your grace's favour, I will take care to ſecure your eſteem.

I am,

My lord,

Your grace's moſt obedient,

and very humble ſervant,

JOHN WILKES.

Gratias tibi, DEUS optime, maxime, cujus nutu & imperio nata eſt & aucta RES ANGLICANA, lubens lætuſque ago, LIBERTATE PUBLICA in hanc diem & horam, per manus, quod voluiſti, meas, ſervatâ, eandem & in æternum ſerva, fove, protege propitiate, ſupplex oro.

www.ingramcontent.com/pod-product-compliance
Lightning Source LLC
Chambersburg PA
CBHW031122020726
47495CB00007B/2312

9783337244040